love and peace

dot-to-dot

love and peace

dot-to-dot

MADDY BROOK

ARCTURUS

ARCTURUS

This edition published in 2016 by Arcturus Publishing Limited
26/27 Bickels Yard, 151–153 Bermondsey Street,
London SE1 3HA

ISBN: 978-1-78599-598-9
CH005191NT

Printed in China

Contents

Introduction

The world is full of so many different and unique people, all with their own stories, cultures and languages, but although we may seem separated, all life on Earth is interconnected.

As the world grows it becomes increasingly important to love one another and to live peacefully. This message can unite us all, but in order to be able to express love and peace to others we must first find it within ourselves. What better way to start than by clearing your mind and focusing on something creative?

Dot-to-dots are a fun and easy way to relax without the stress of time pressure. They are also a great way to create a wonderful image without requiring any drawing experience. All you have to do is connect the dots that are consecutively numbered.

There are more than 120 images in this book all depicting scenes, words, symbols, objects and people from around the world that are representative of either love or peace. After finishing one of these puzzles, the user will have their own lovely illustration to keep.

So, settle down with a nice sharp pencil or pen and get ready to open your mind, and your heart, with these delightful dot-to-dot puzzles.

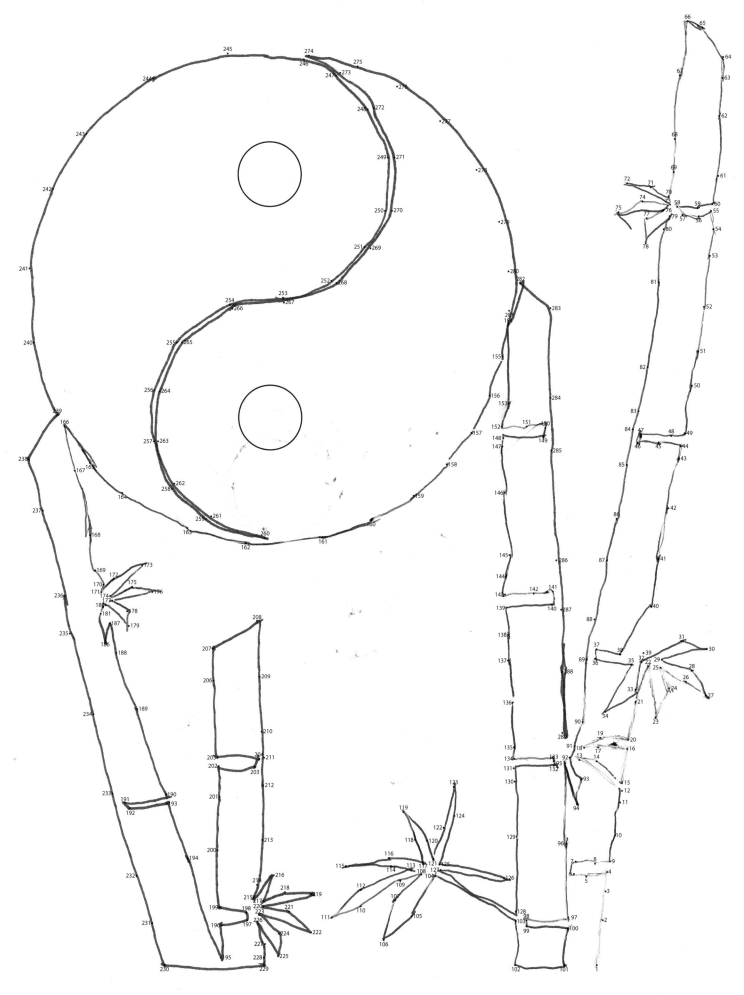

8

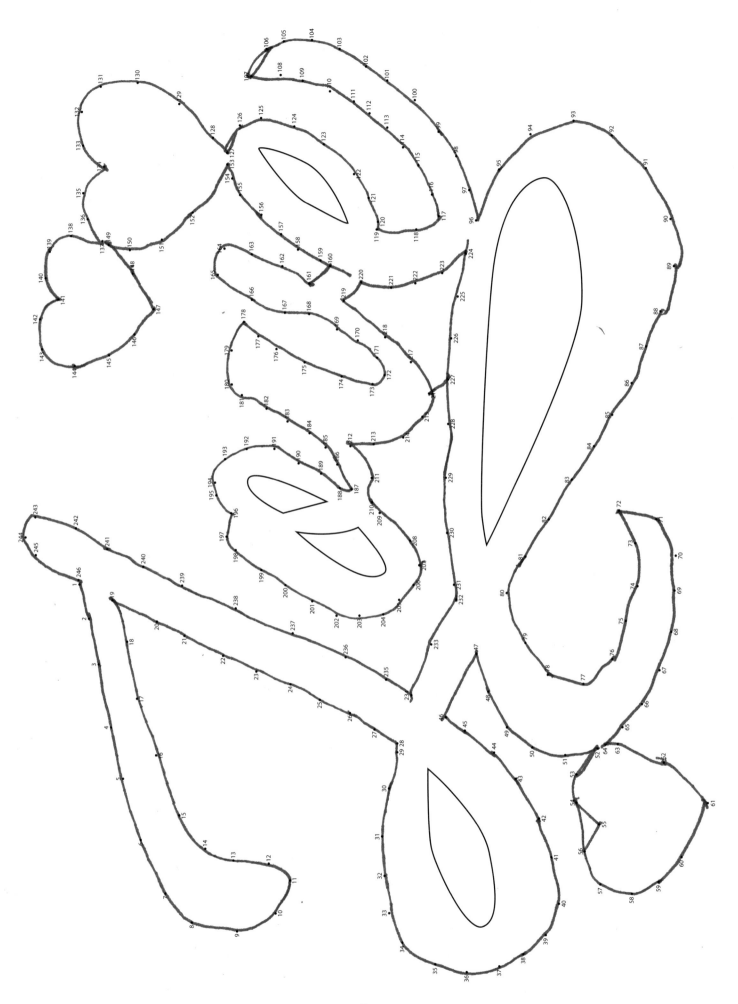

9

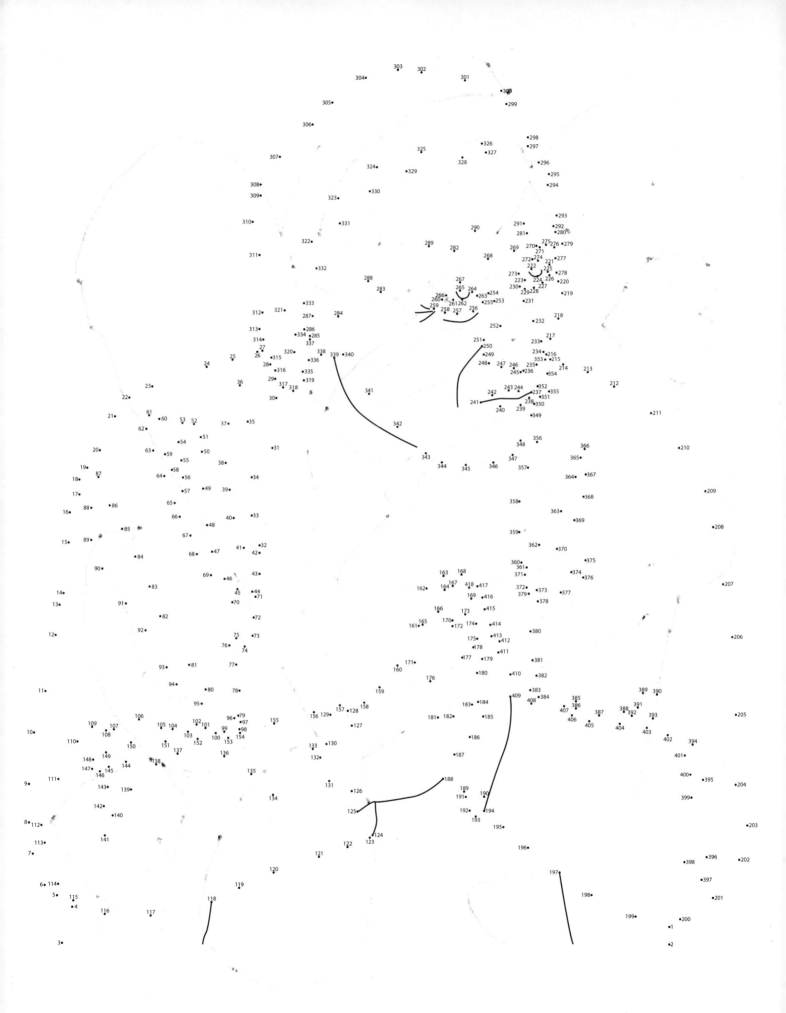

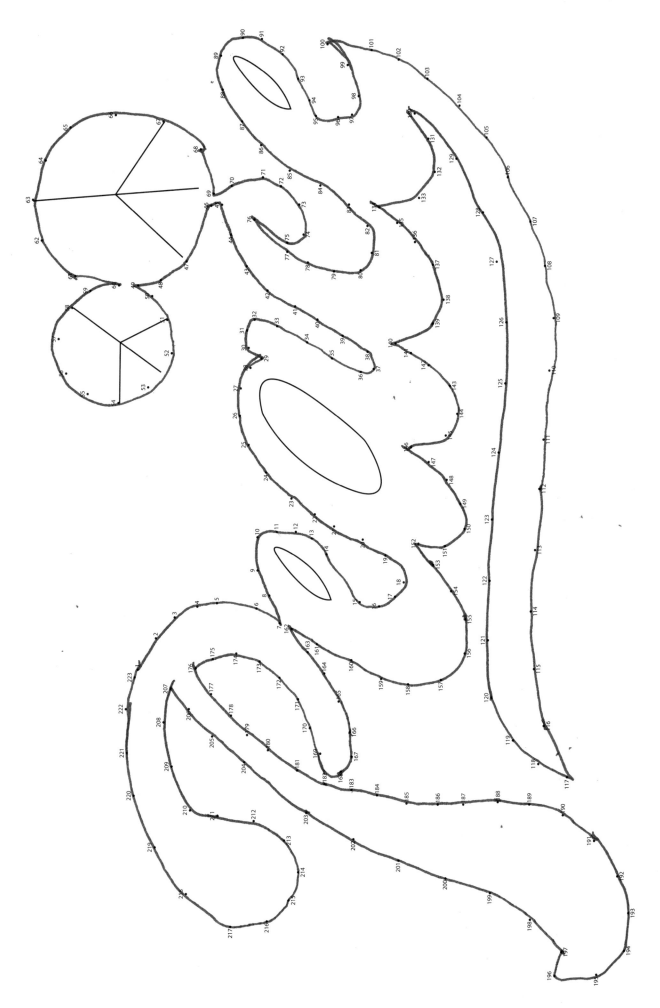

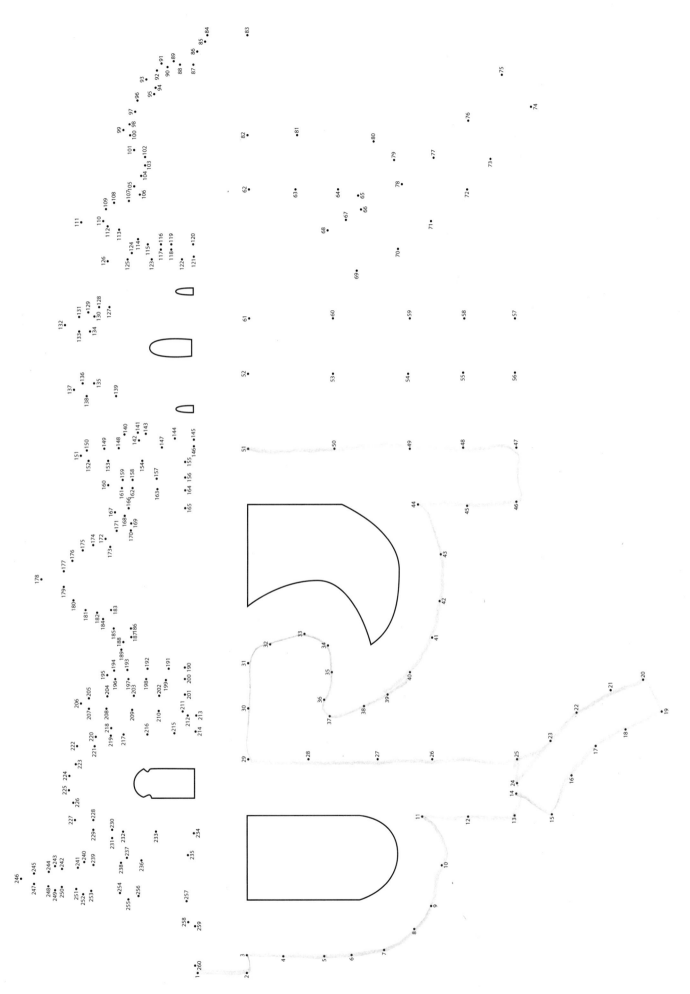

13

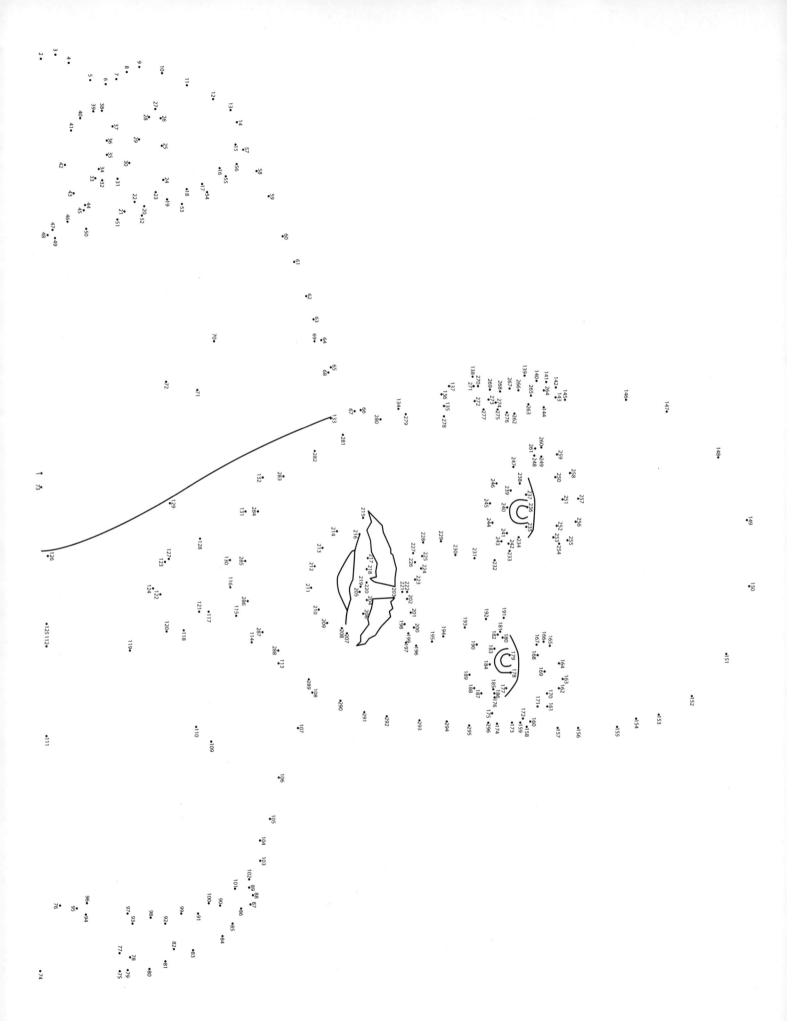

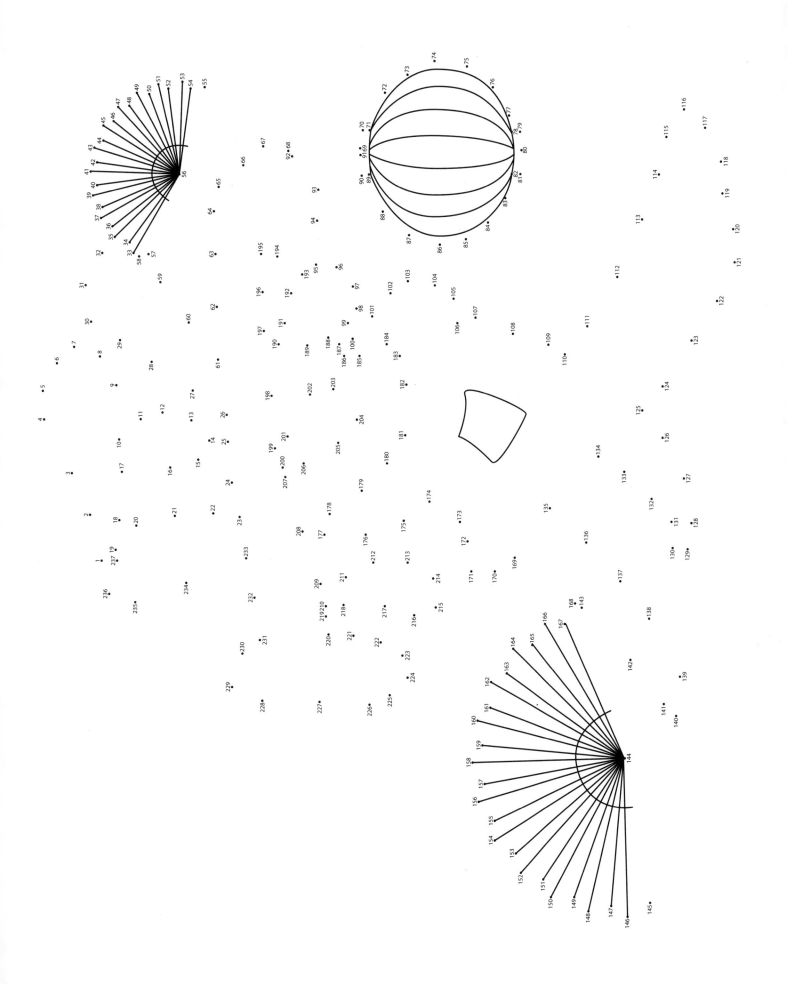

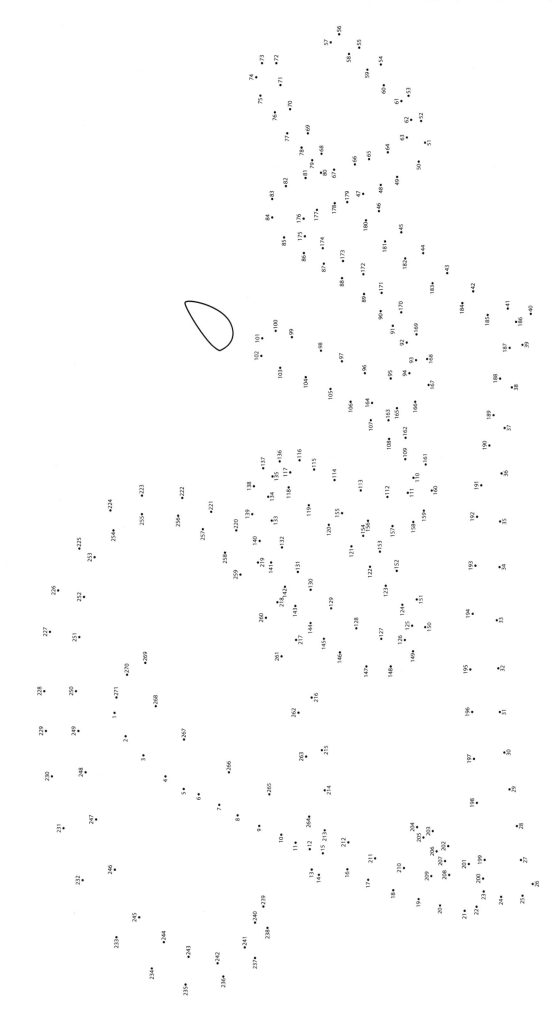

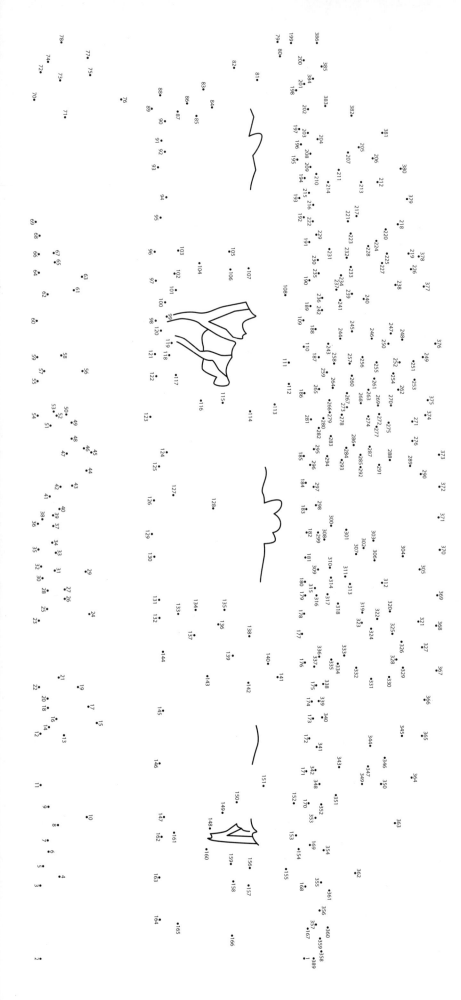

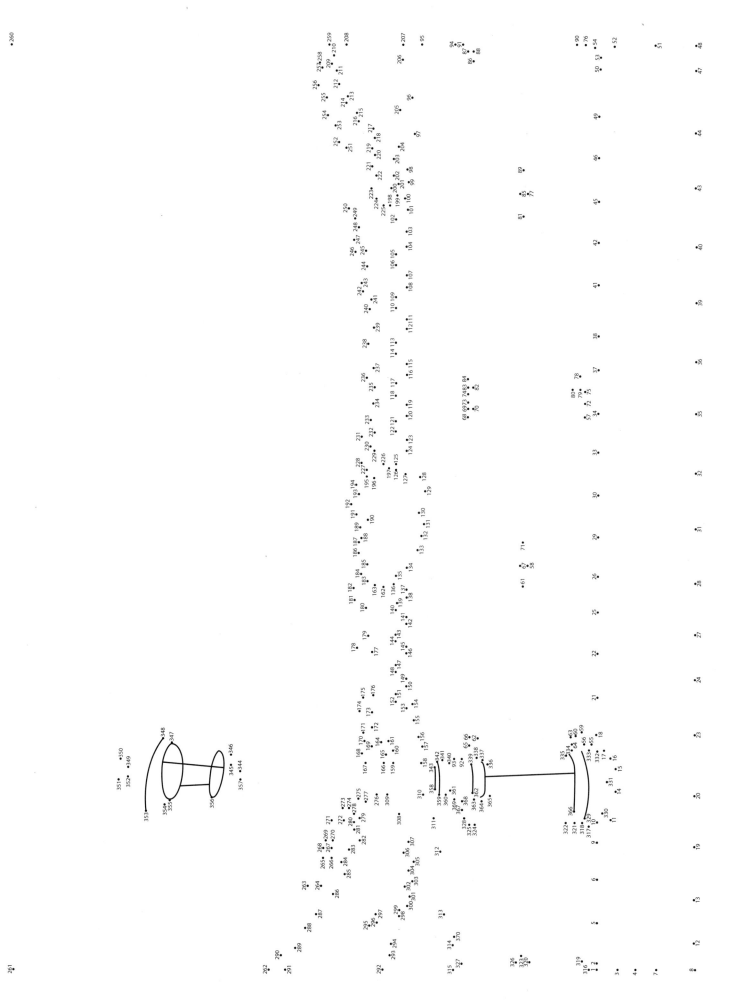

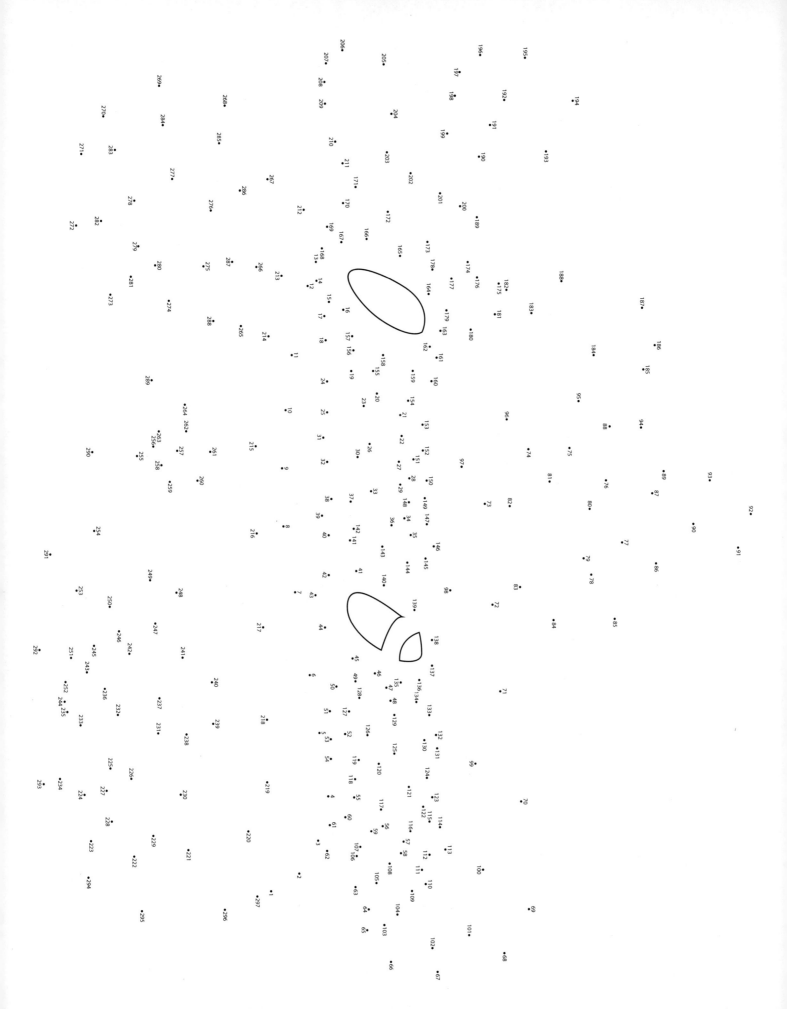

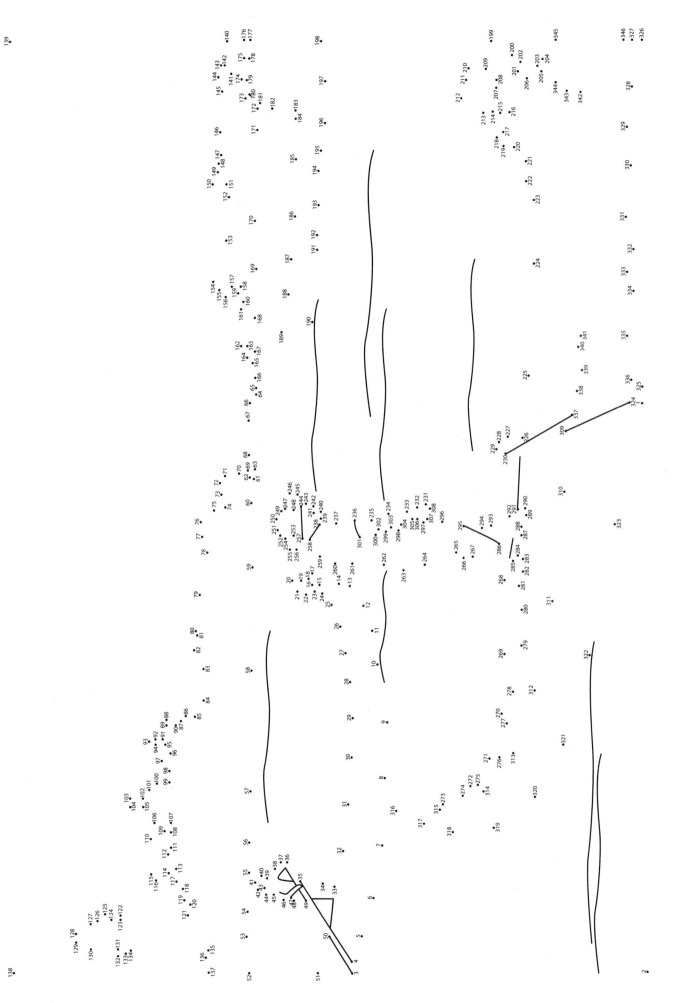

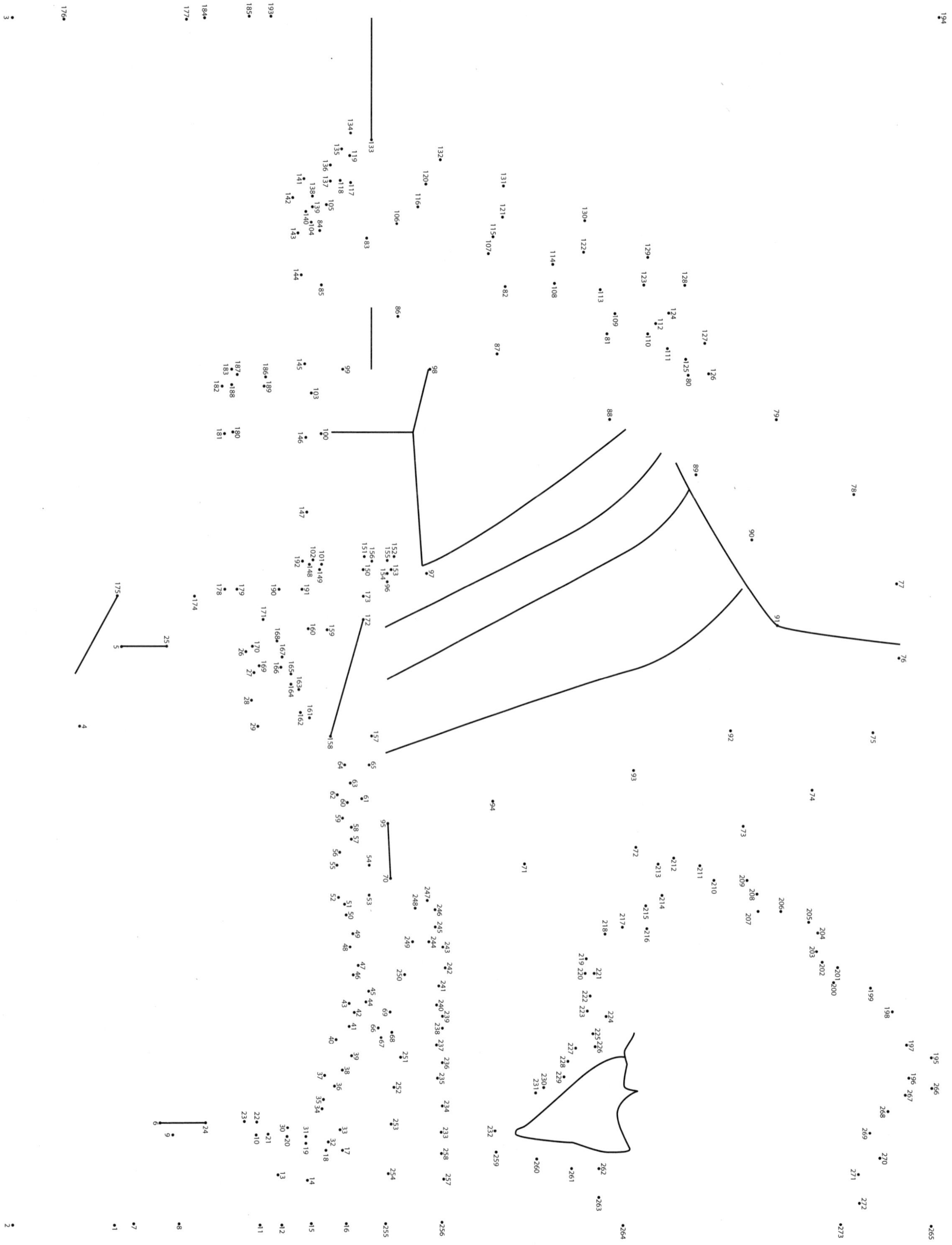

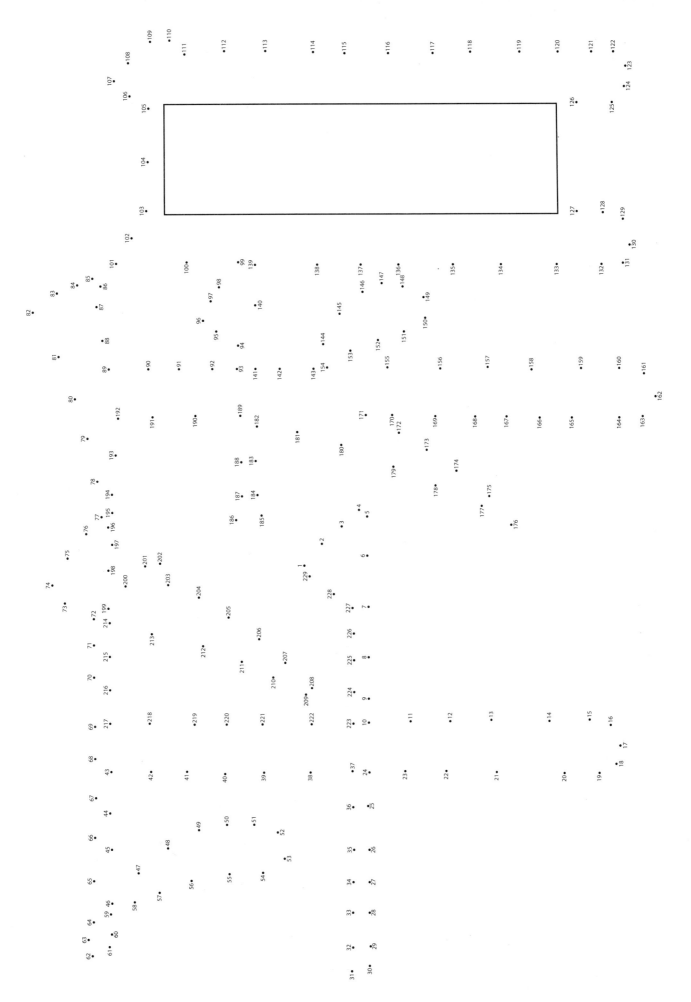

23

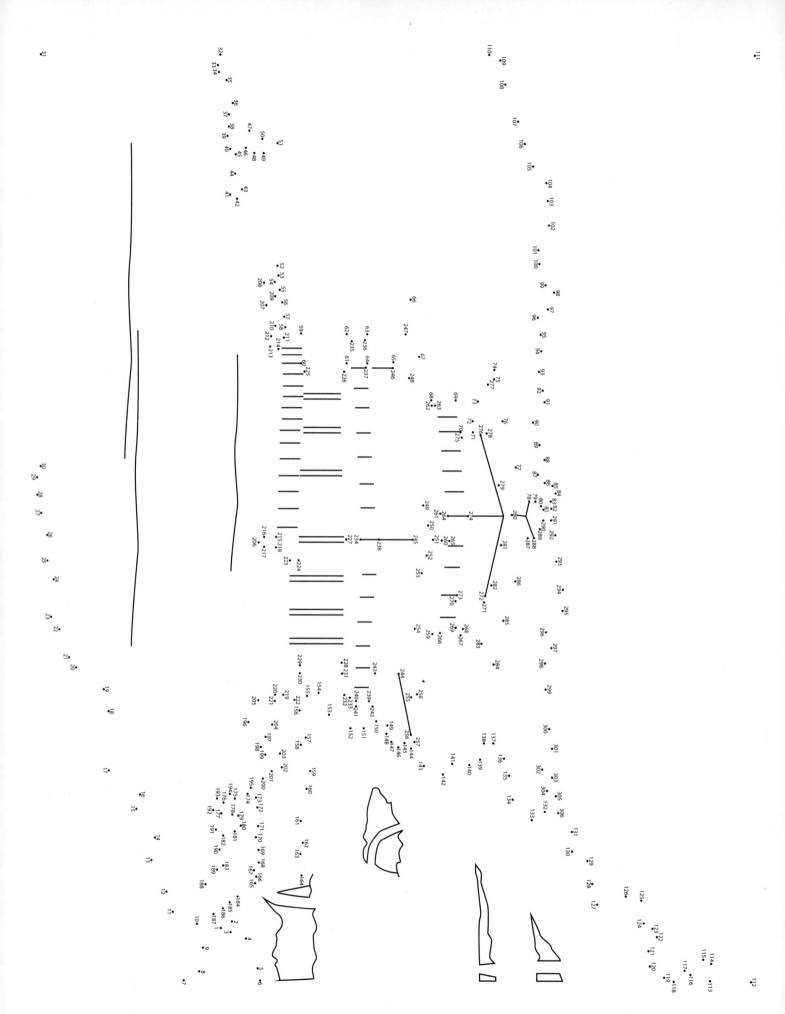

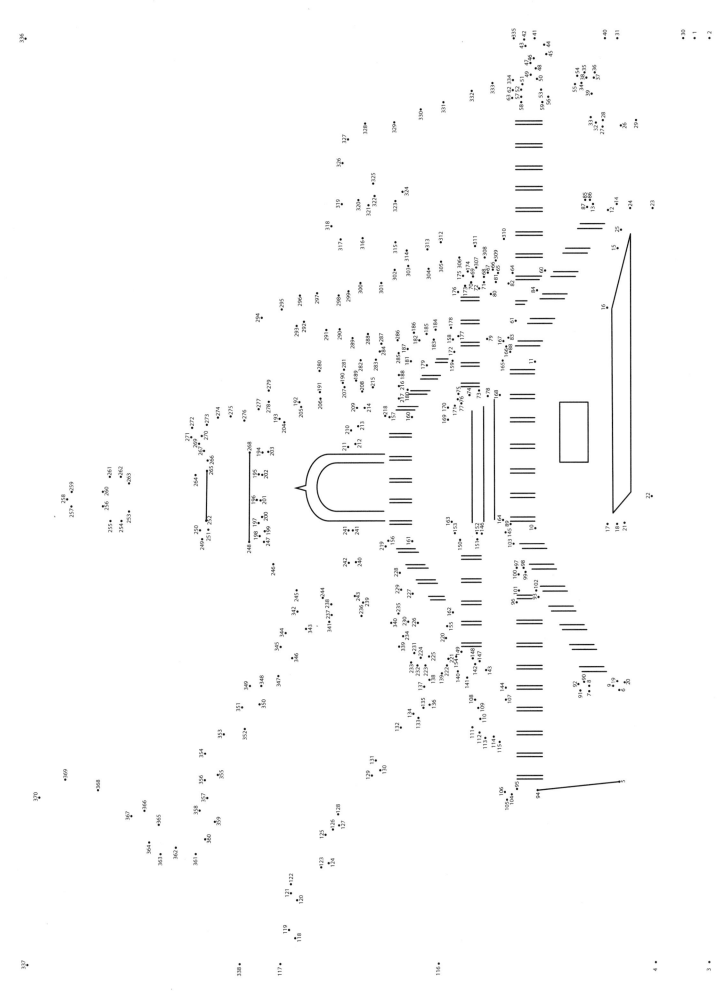

25

26

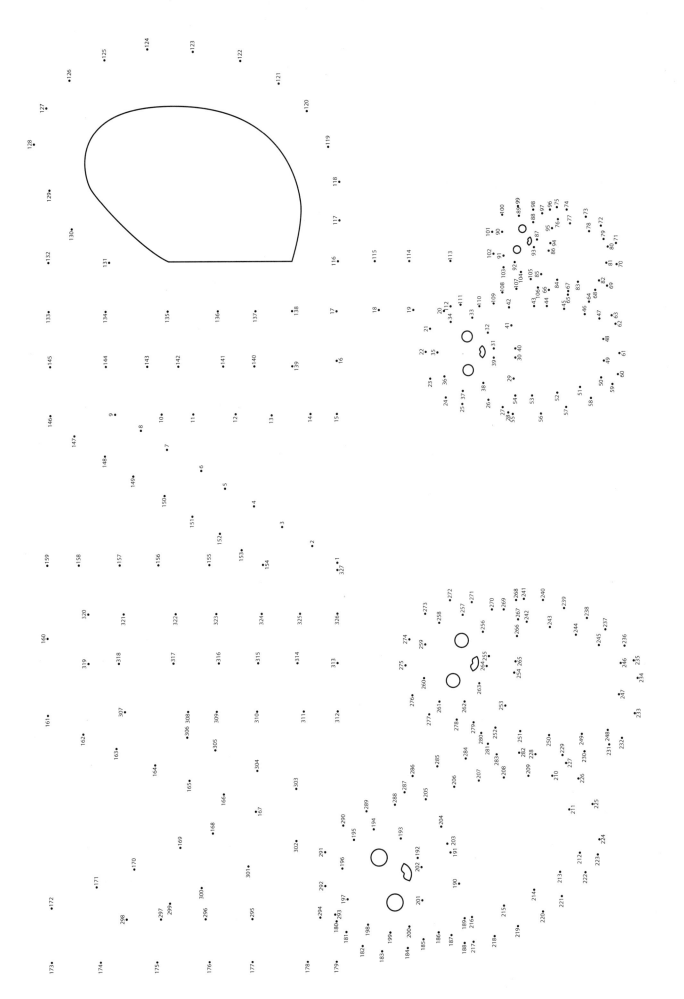

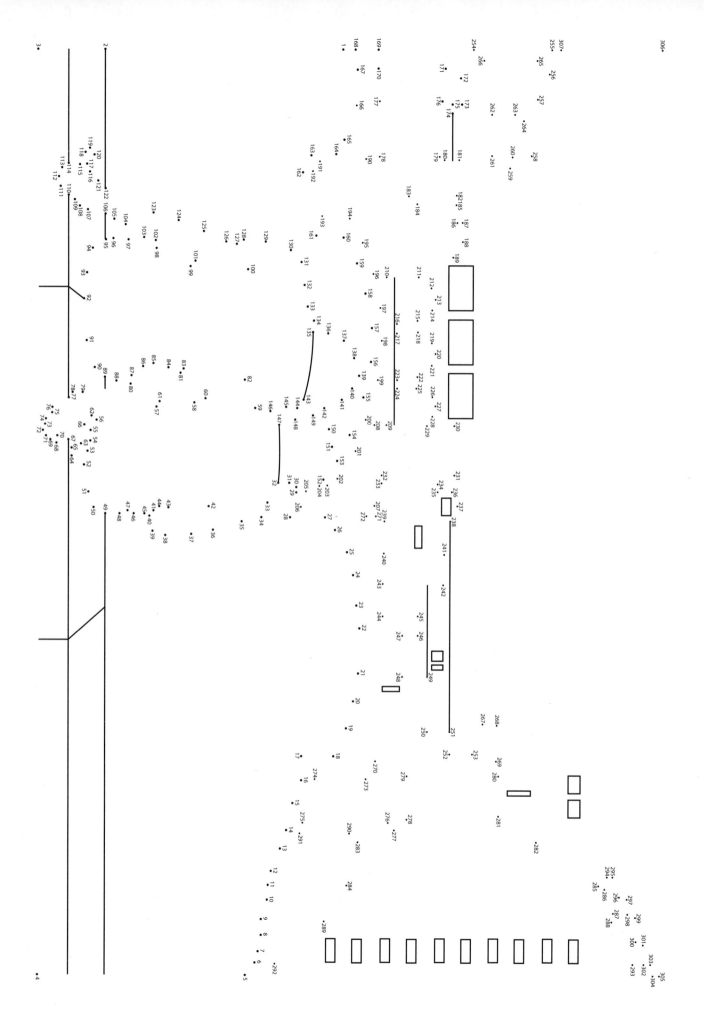

28

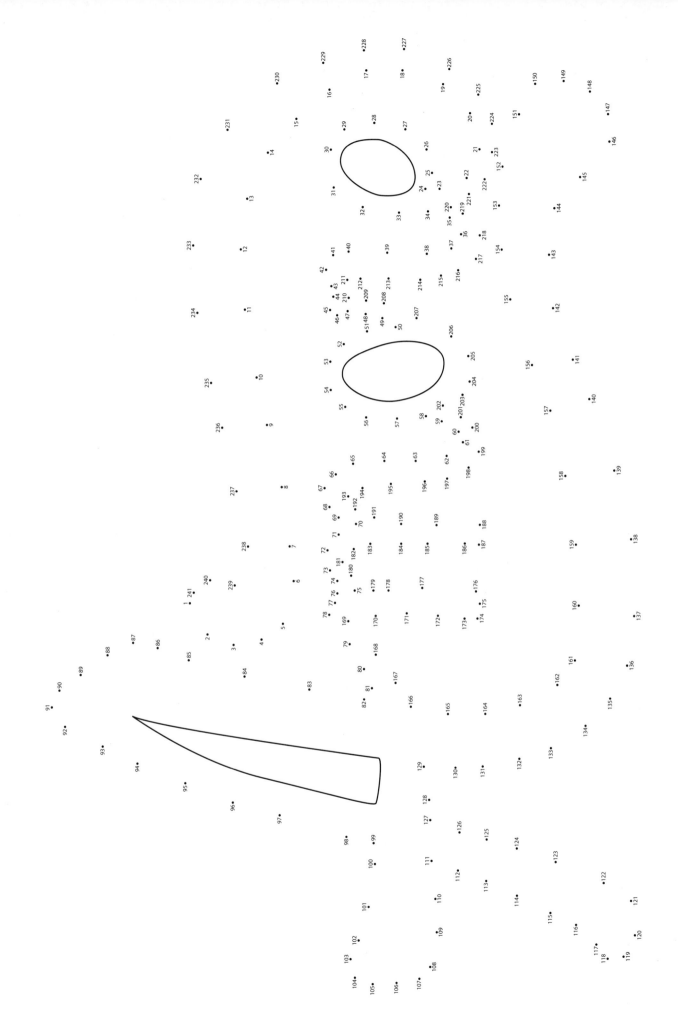

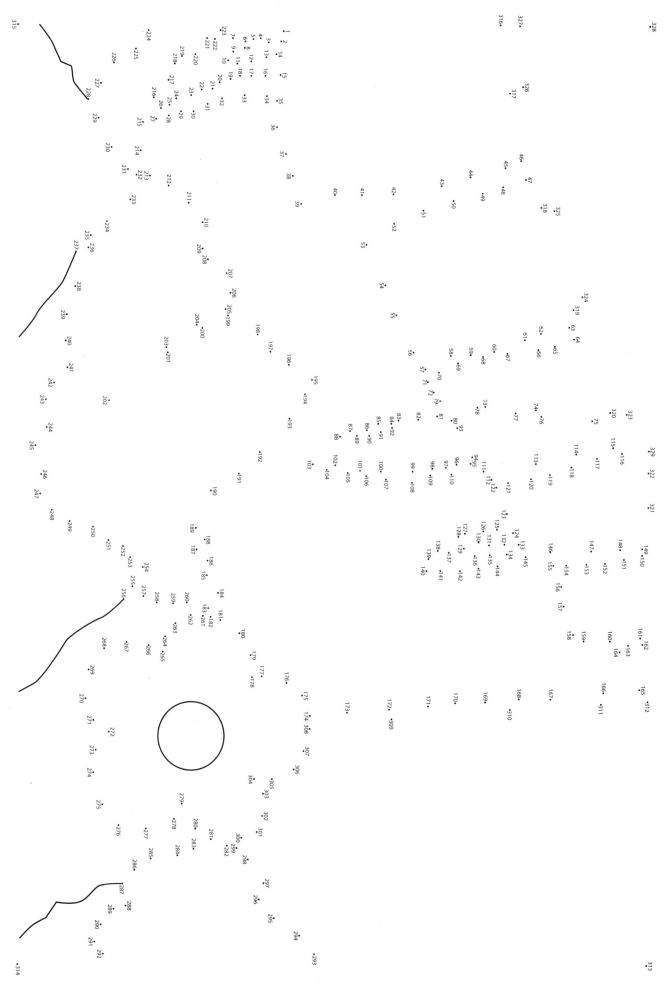

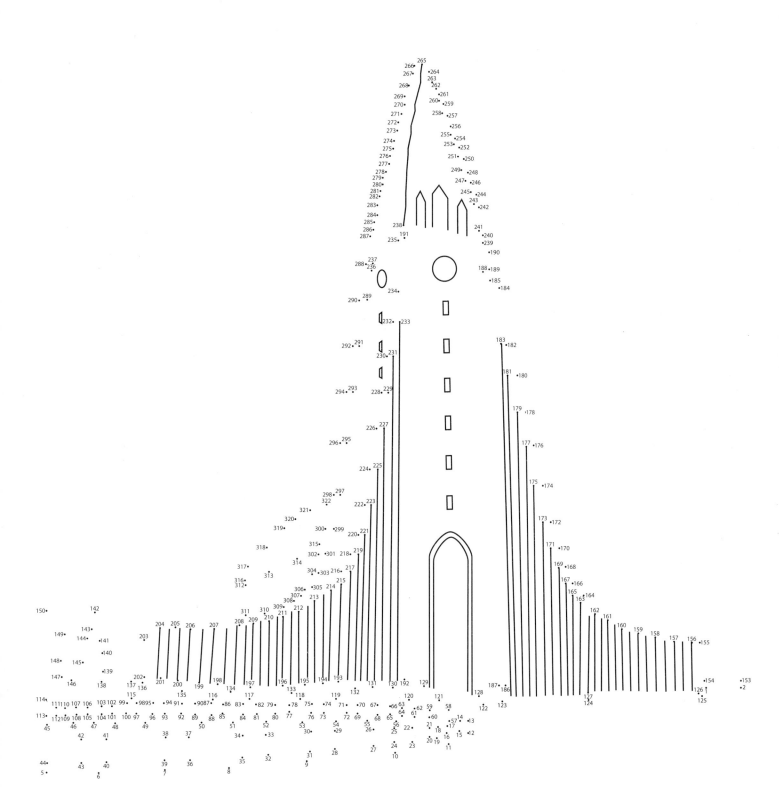

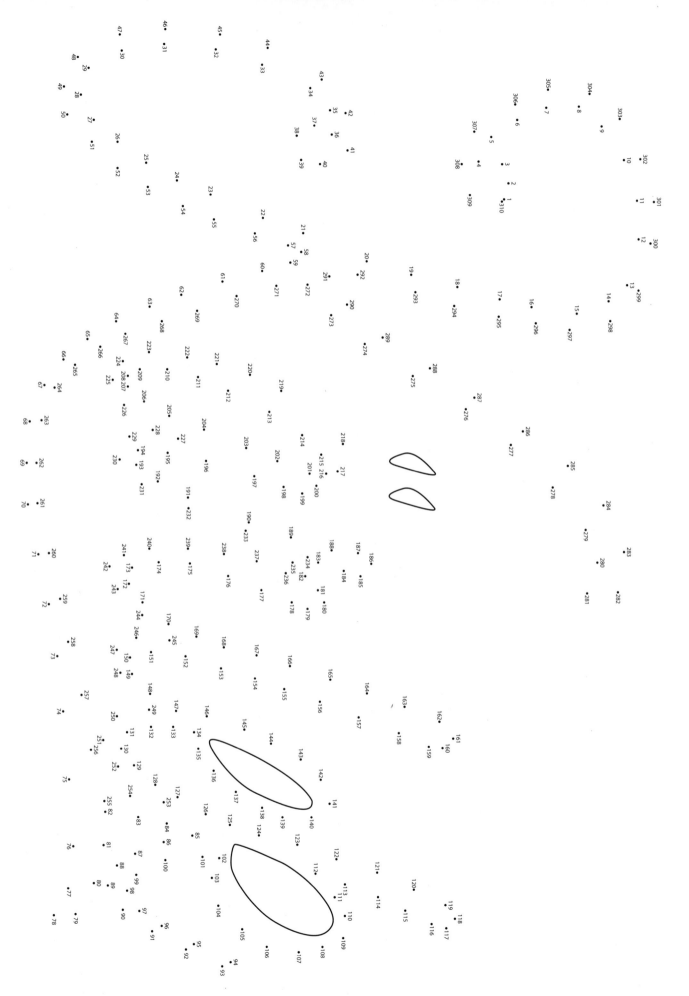

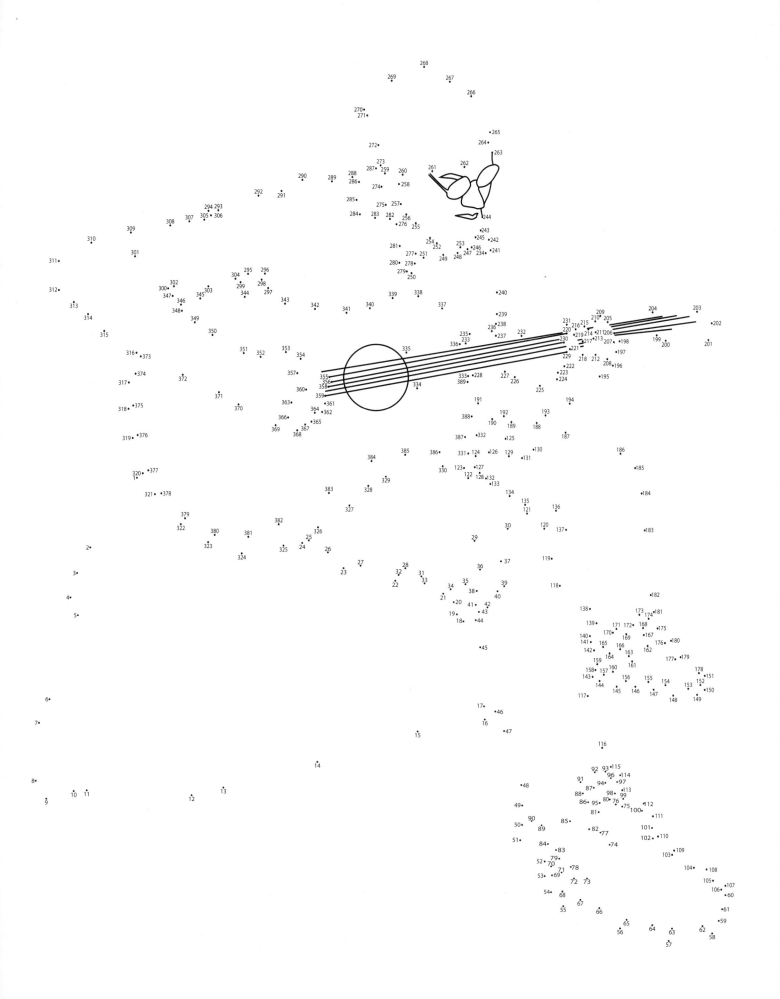

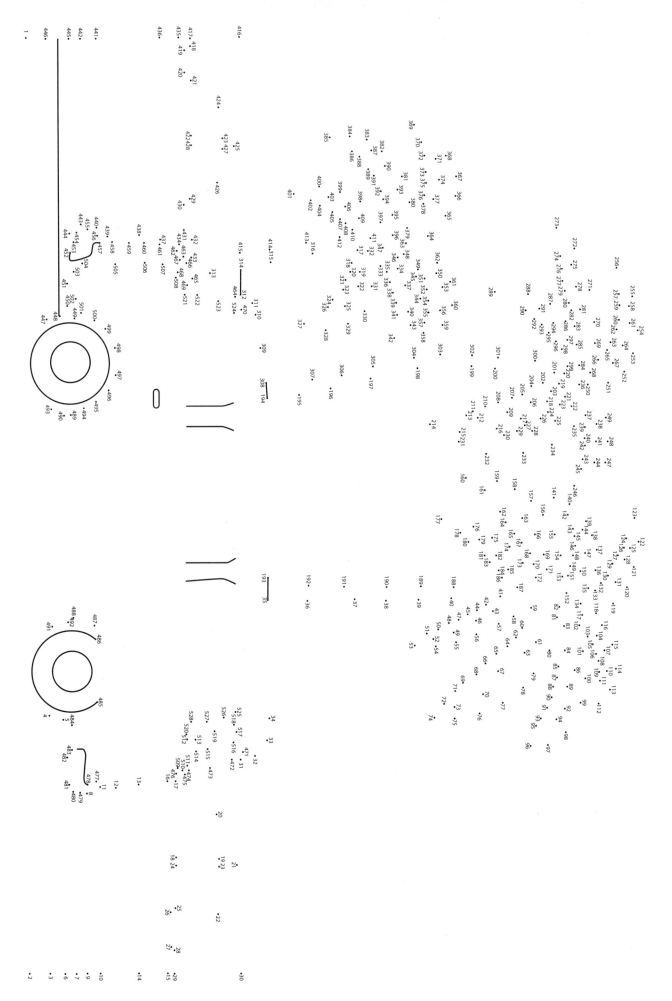

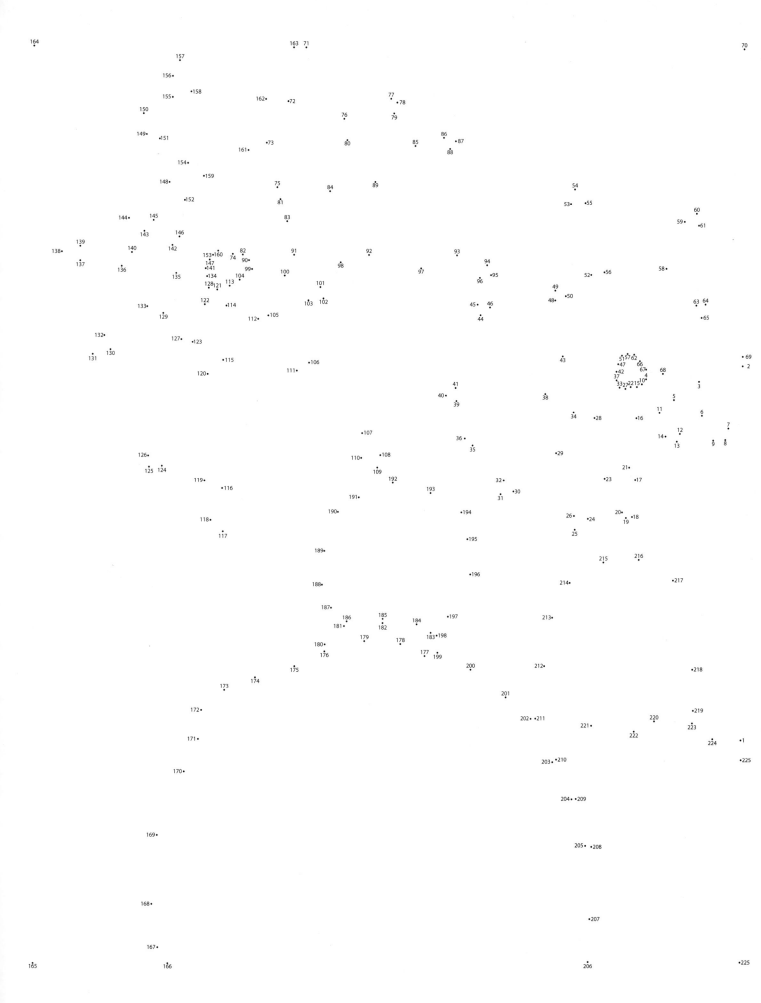

35

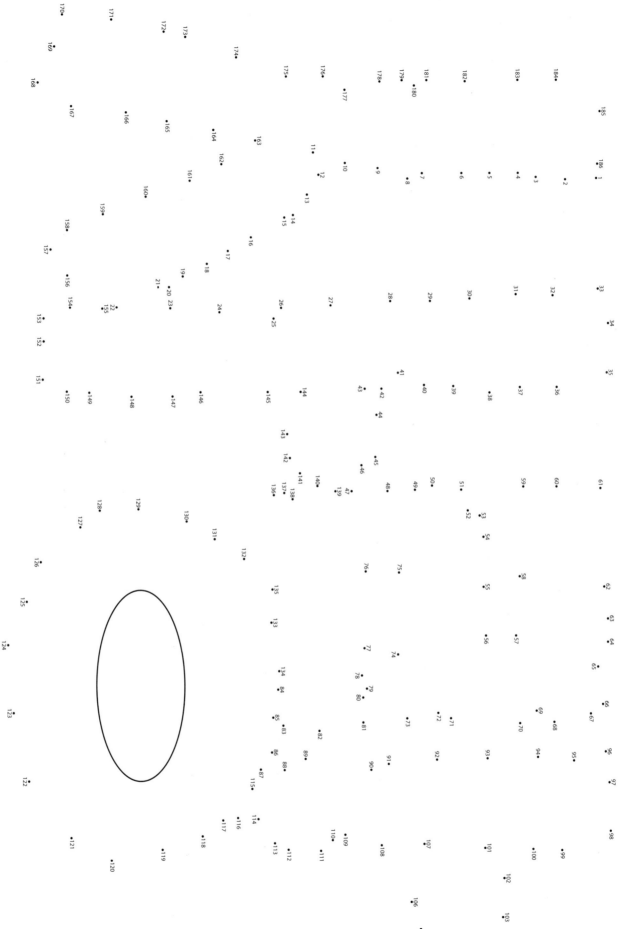

38

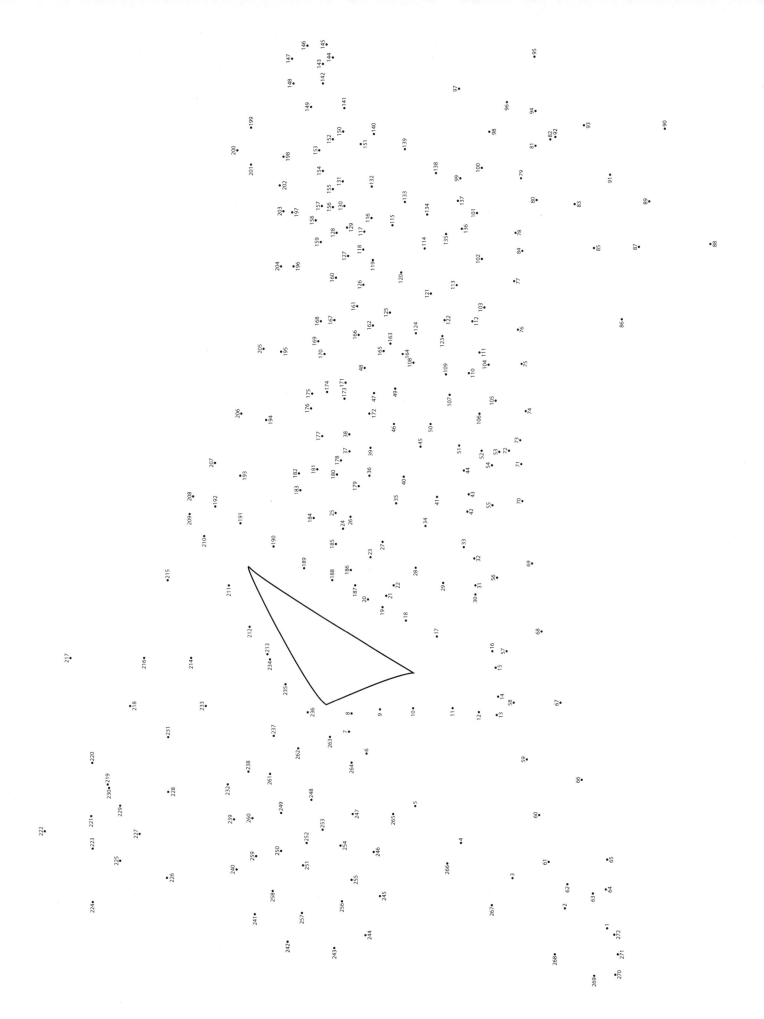

40

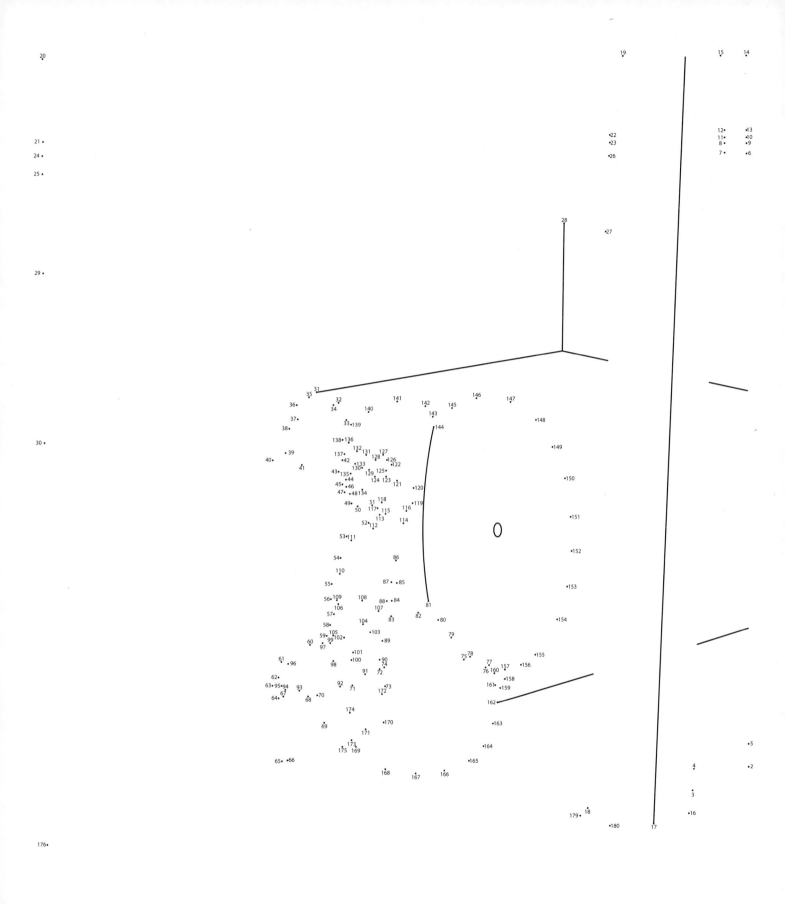

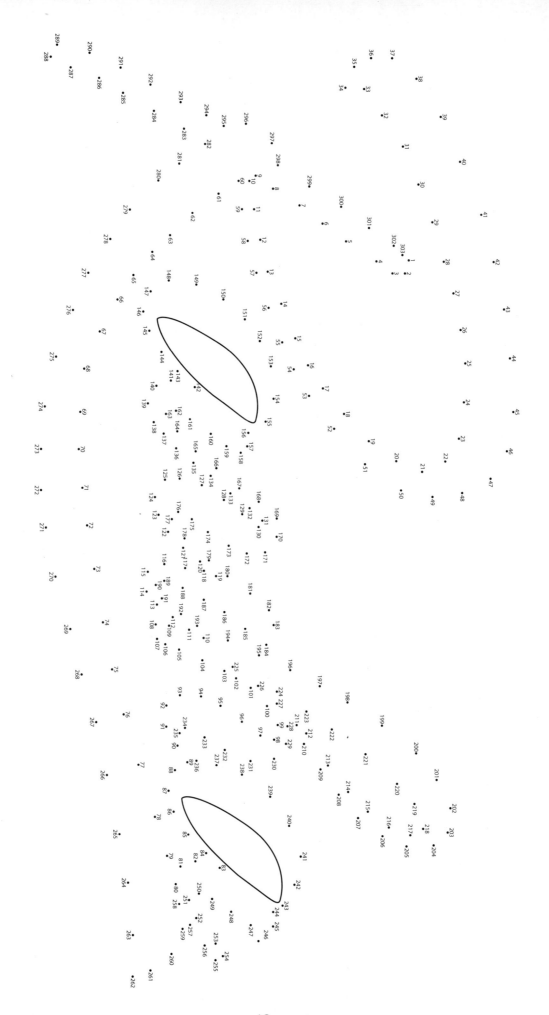

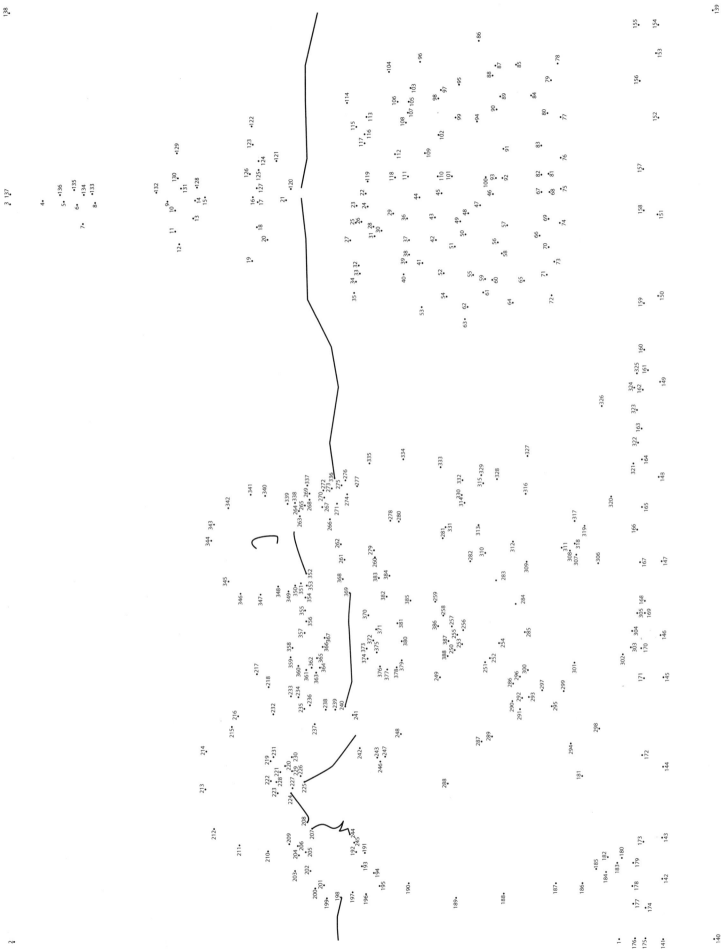

43

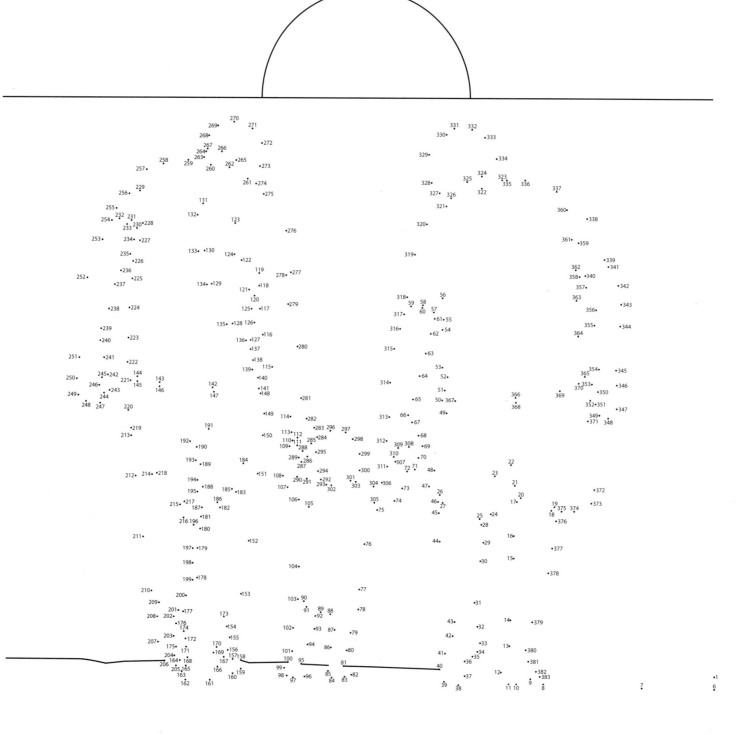

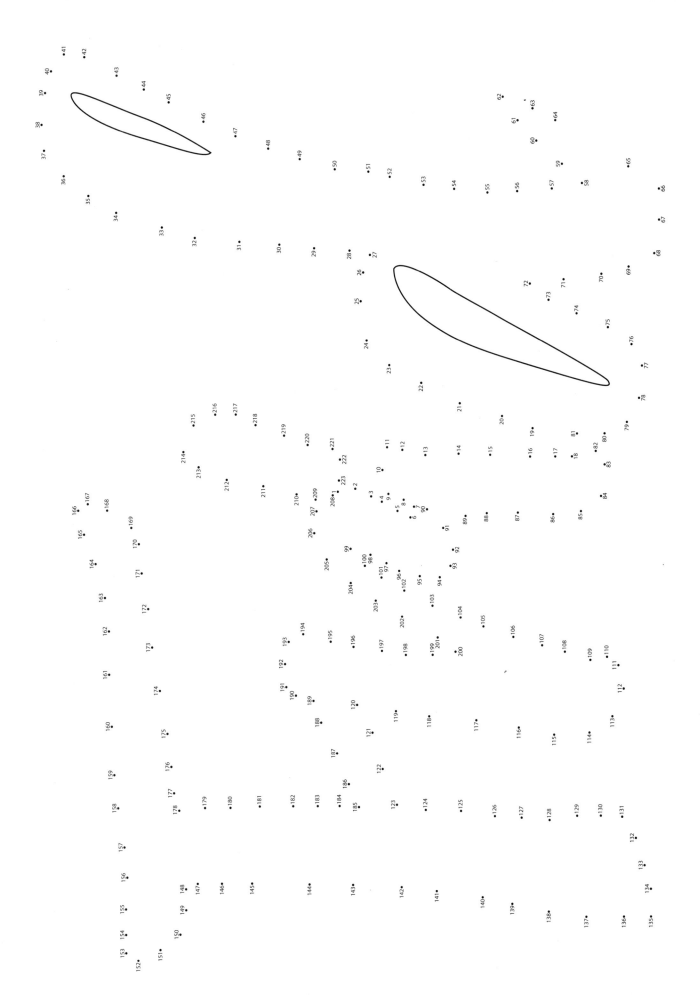

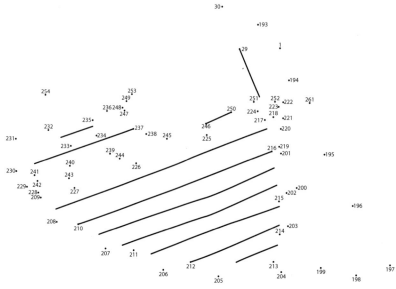

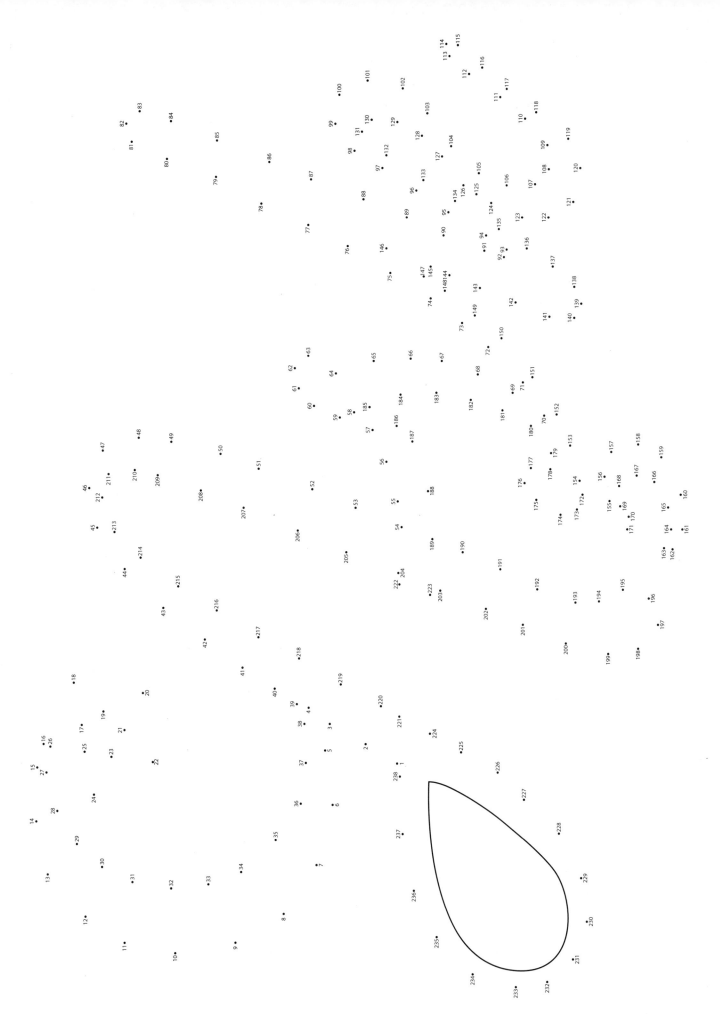

47

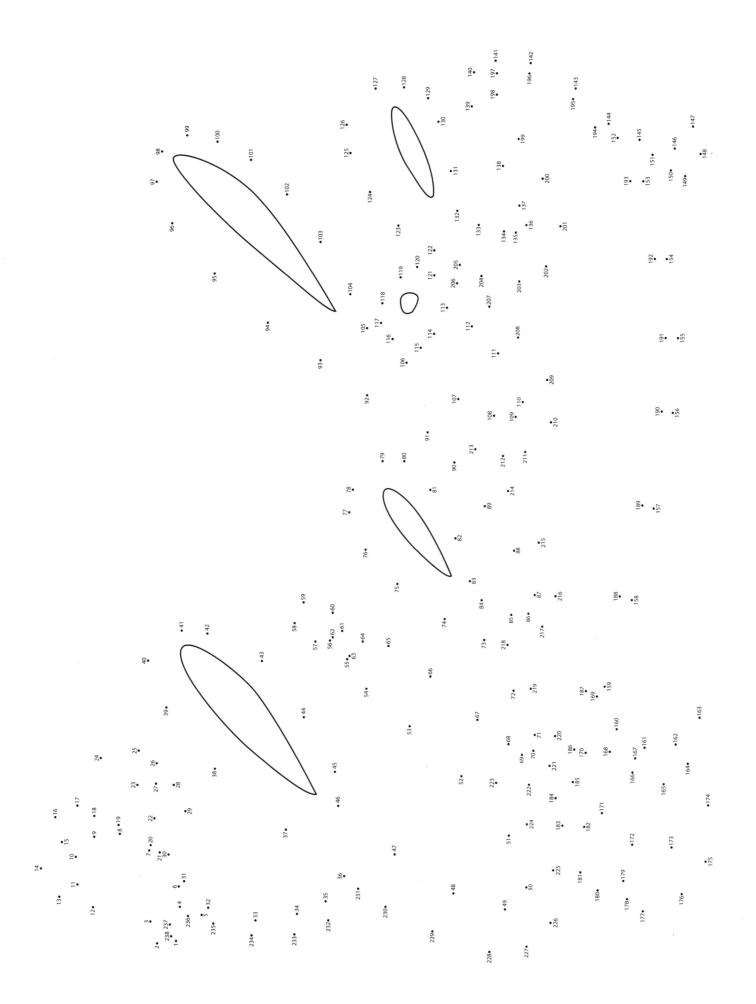

49

50

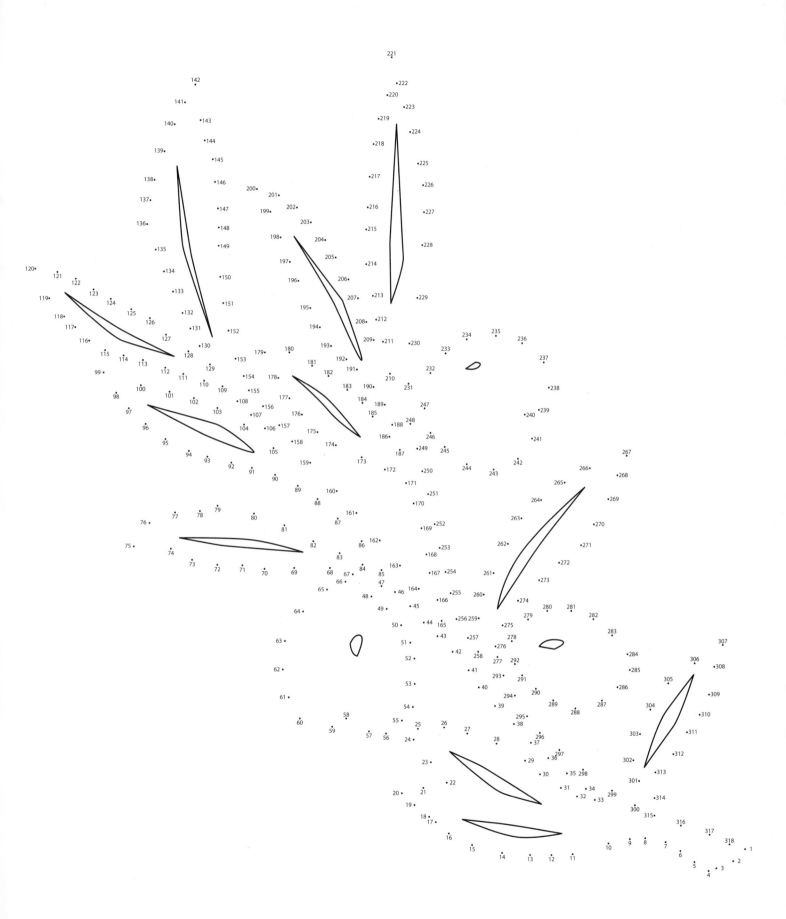

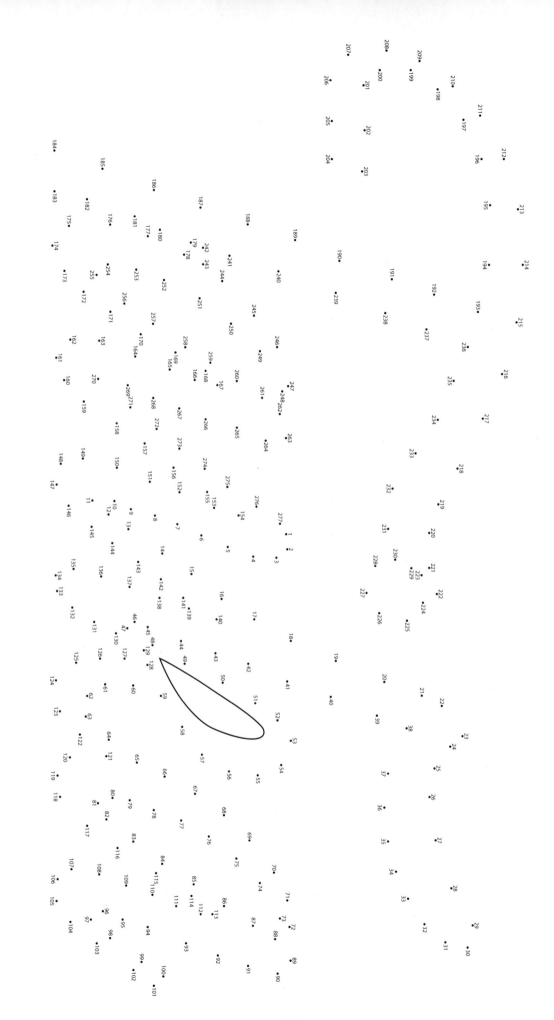

52

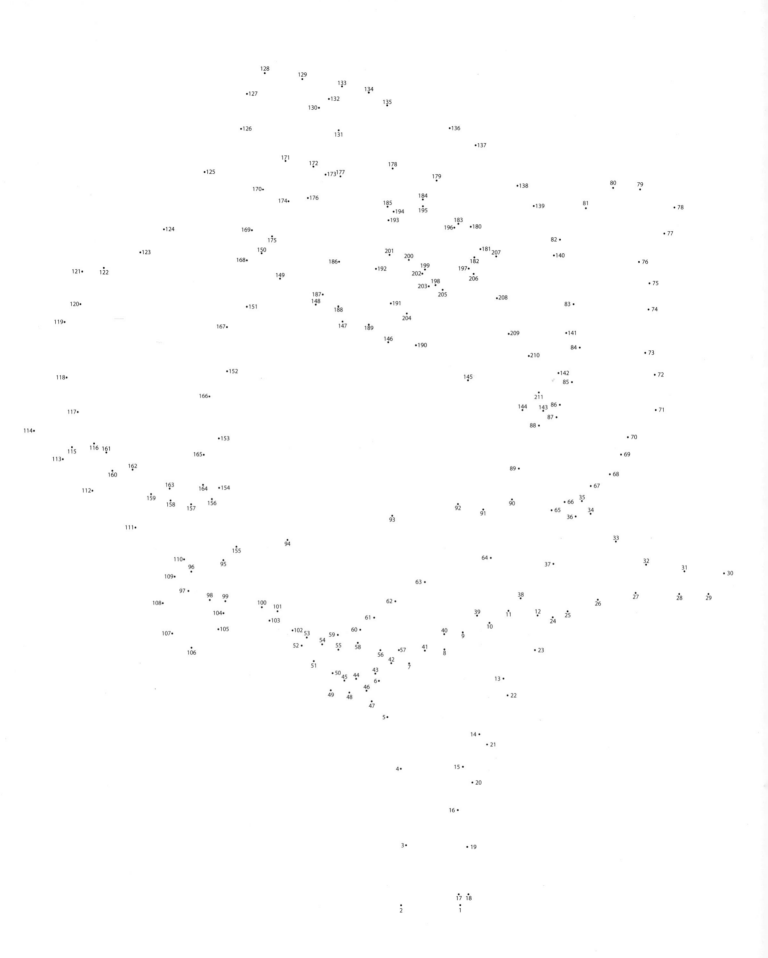

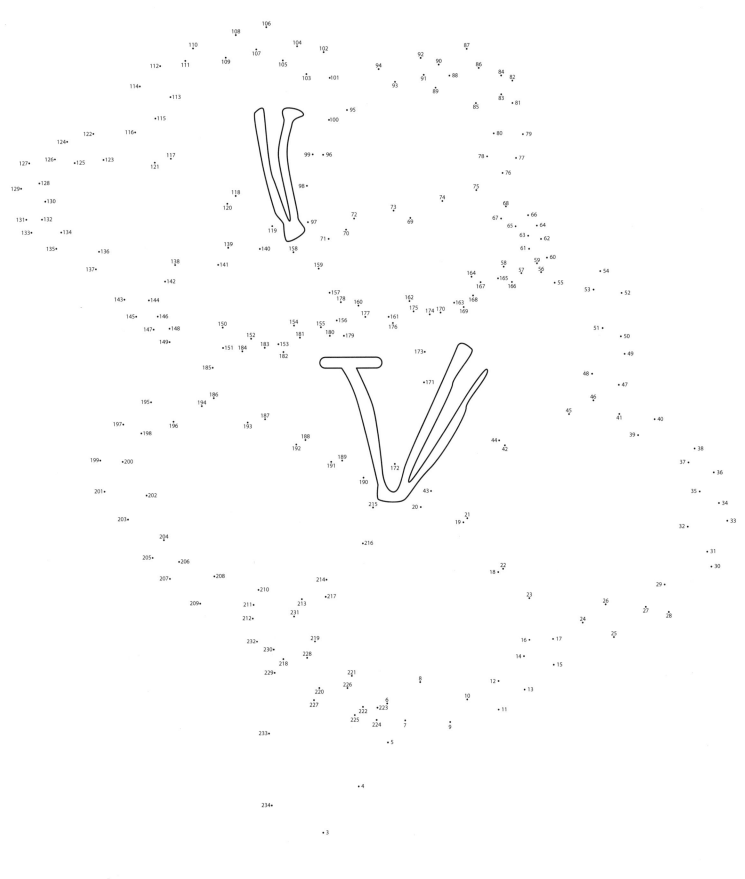

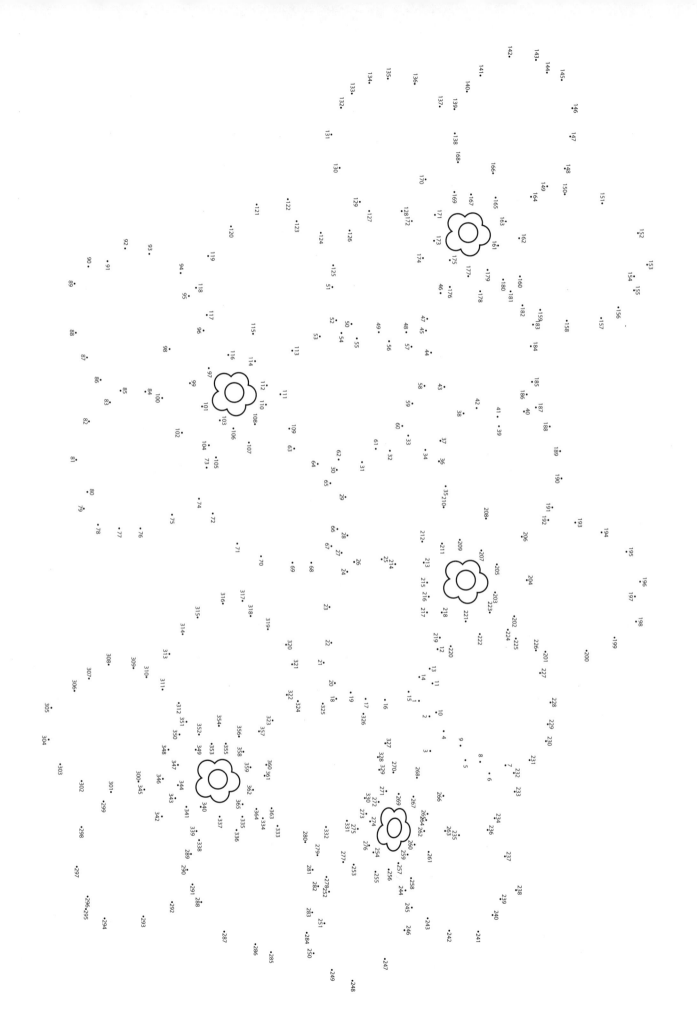

58

161 162
160
163
164
165
159
158 166
143 144
142 167
157 168
141
145
140 156
169
155 170 173
154 171 172 174
146
139 147 149 153
137 138 148 150 152 175
136
151
55
56
135
54
177
134 57
53 178
58
104 133 52 179
59
51
132 60 180
50
103 61
105 181
102 49
131 182
62
48 183
130 63
47 184
185
64 46
99 108 186
45 187
65 188
98 109 44 1
110 66
43 2
97 128 67 42 3
111 127 41 4
96 112 68 5
126
95 113 40 6
125 69 39
94 73 7
114 38 23
124 75 72 22
74 70
93 115 123 71 37 24 21 8
76 9
77
92 116 122 25 10
78 36 20
91 79 26 11
117 35 19
121 34 27 12
90 80 18
118 81 28 13
89 120 33
82 17
88 32 29 14
119 83
87 86 85 84 31 30 16 15

61

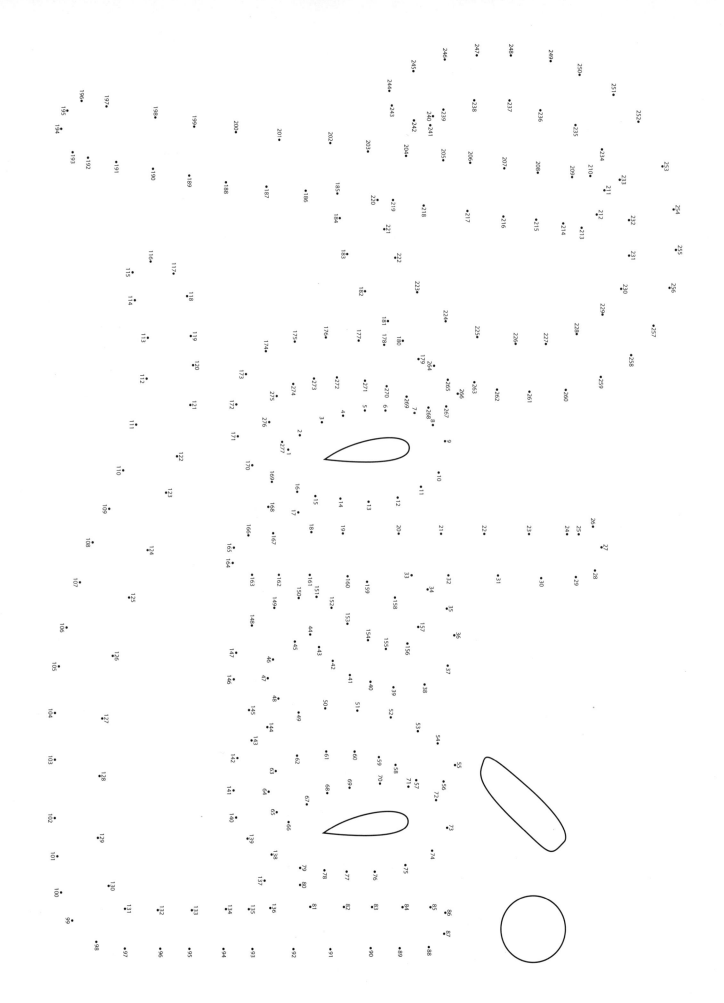

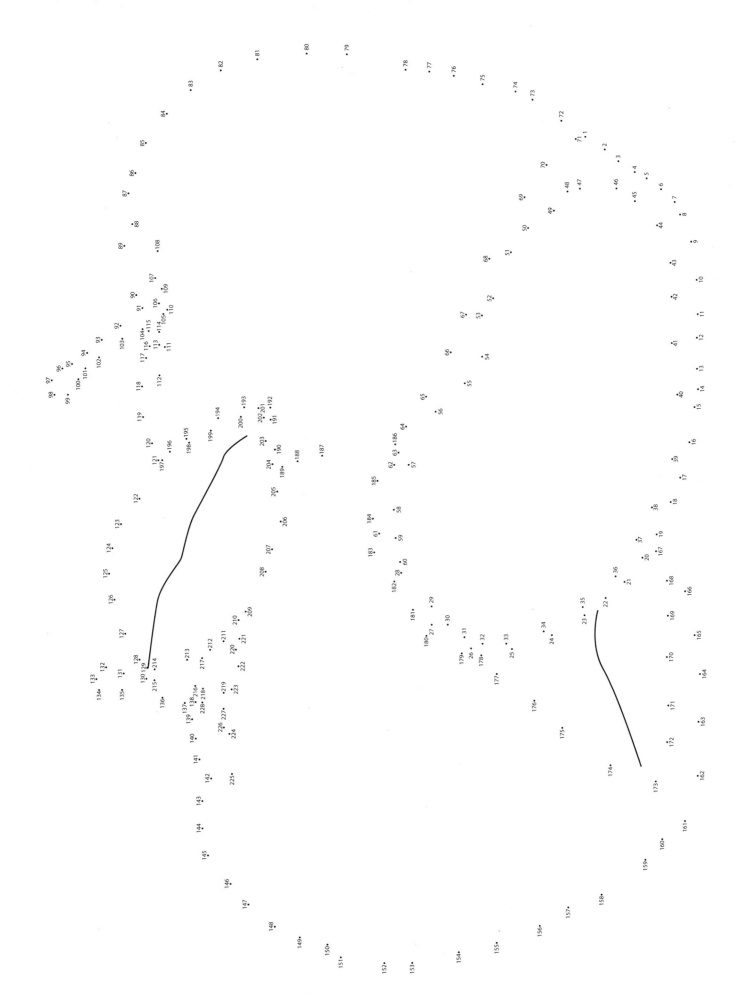

63

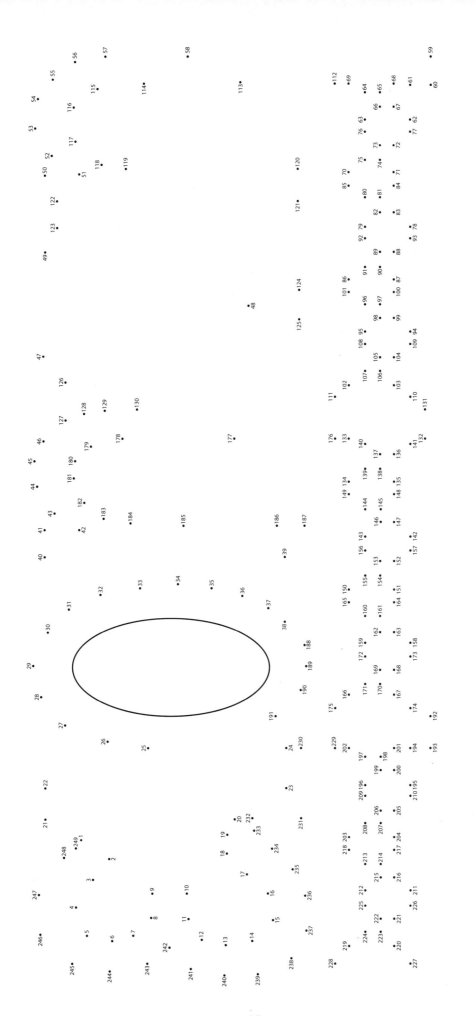

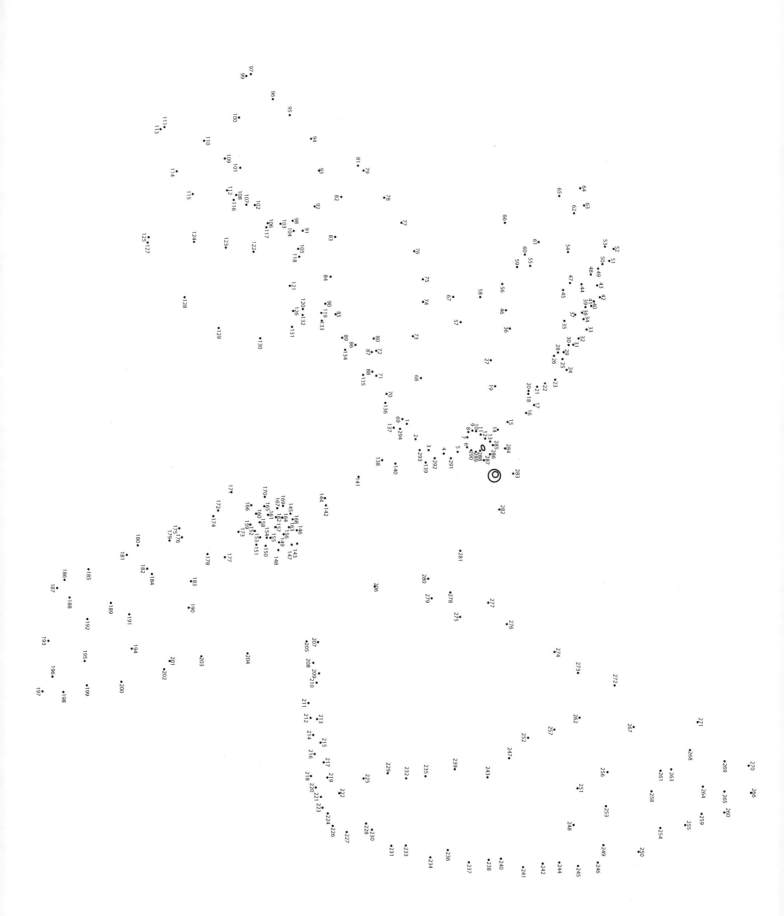

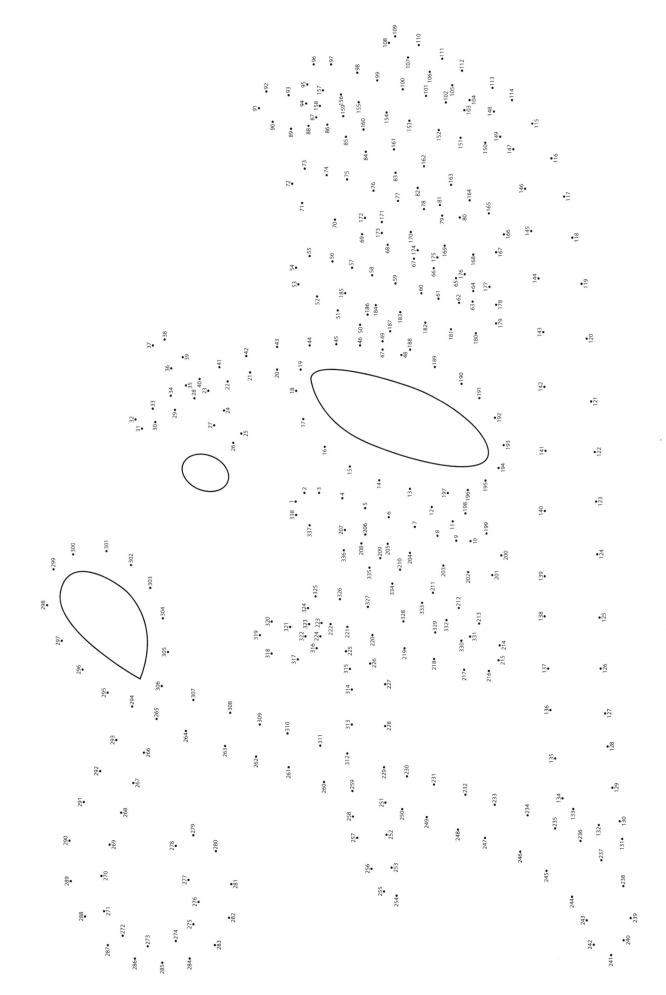

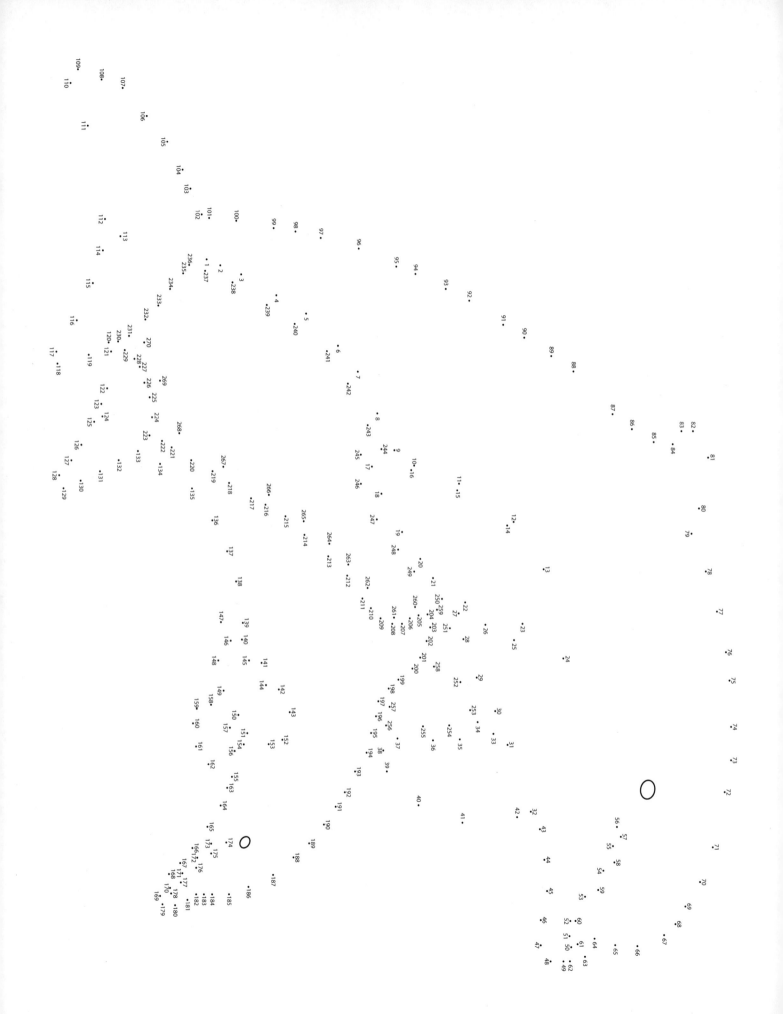

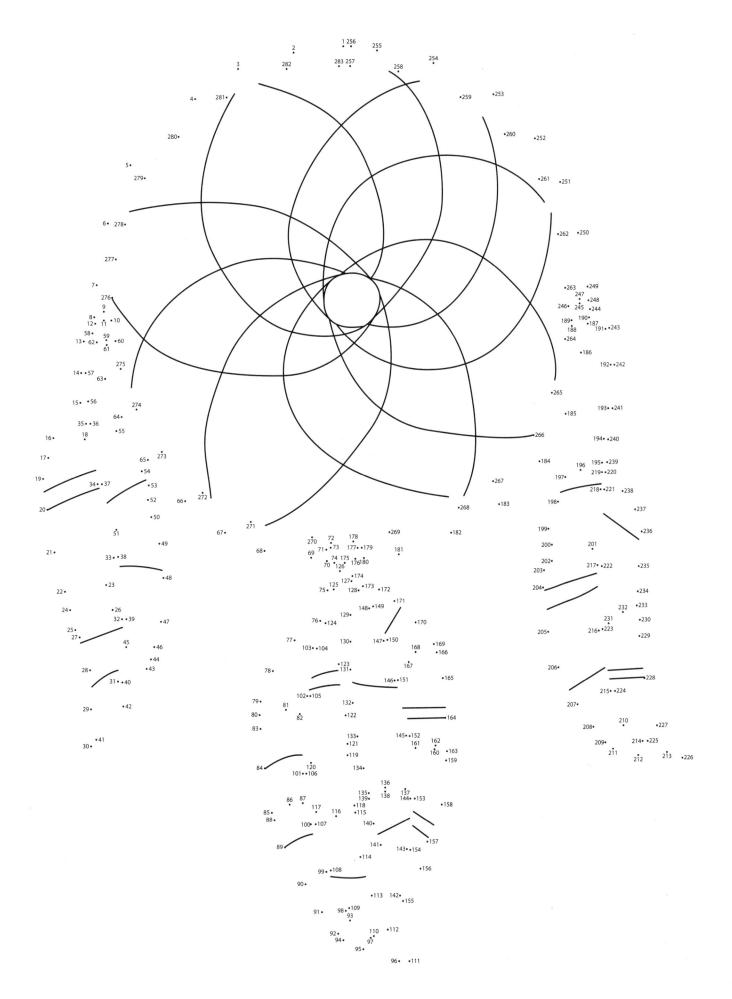

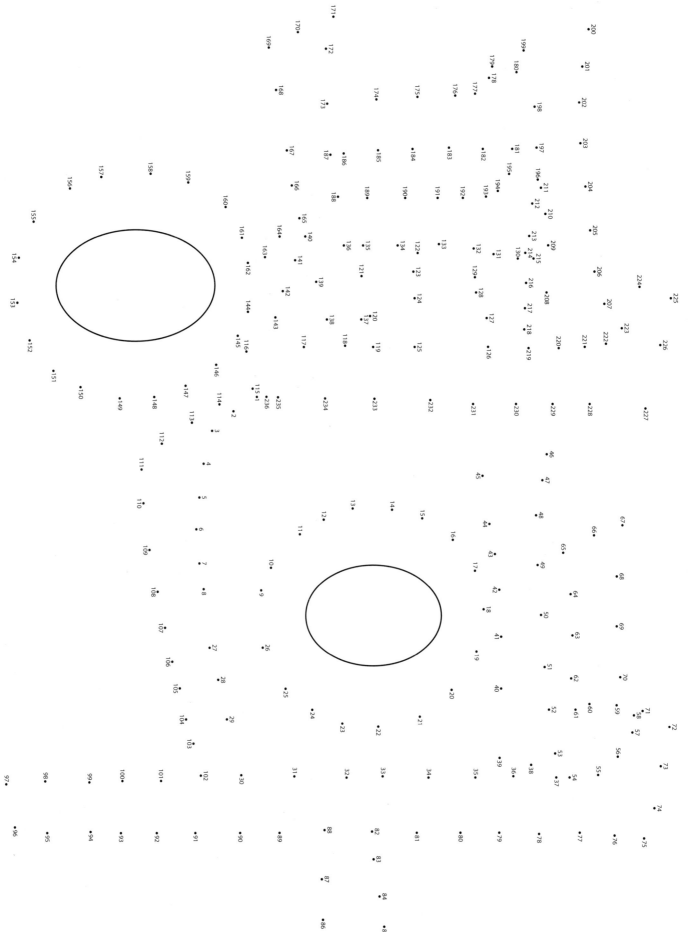

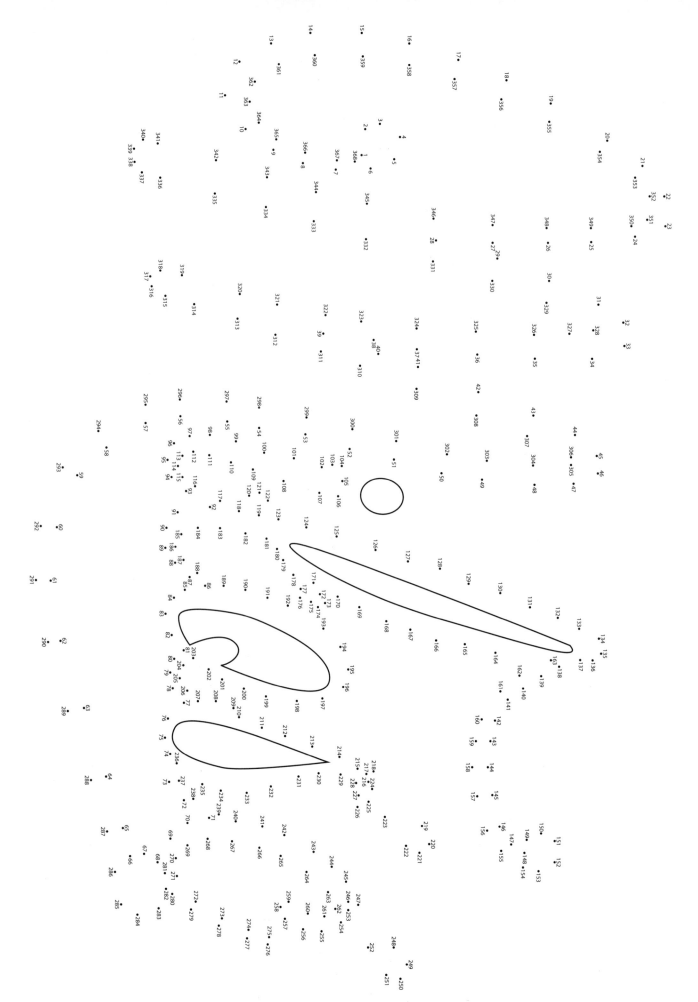

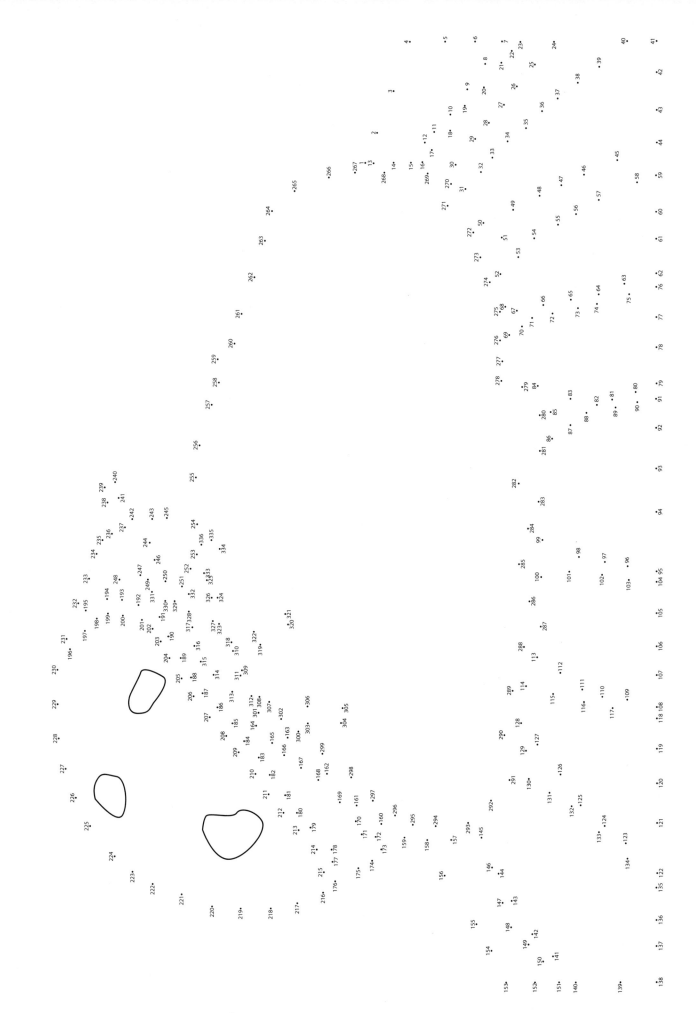

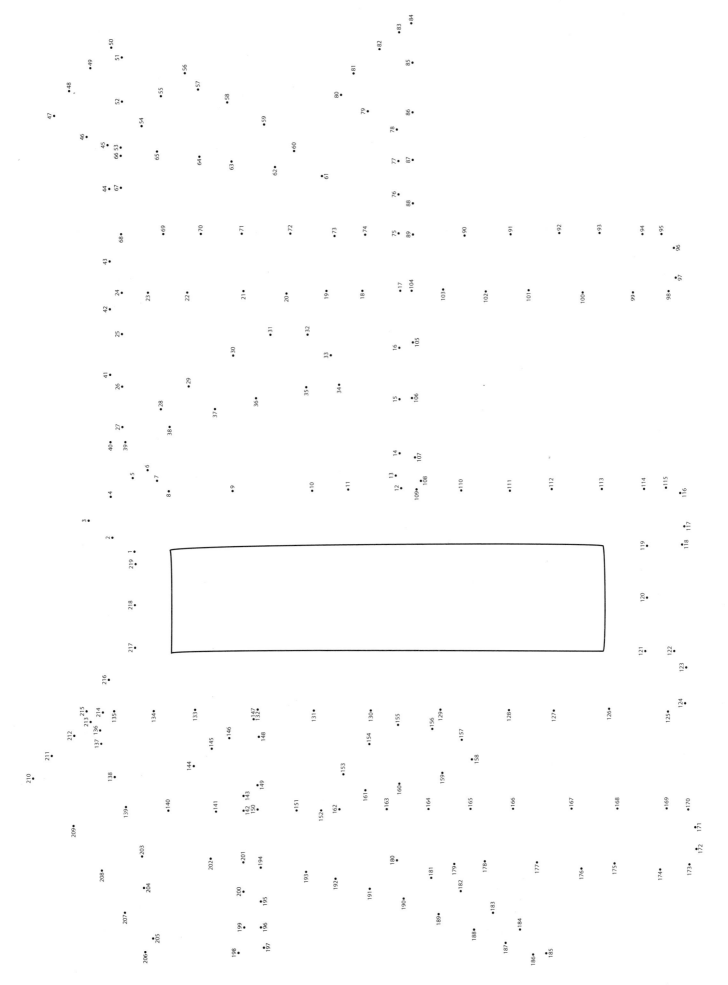

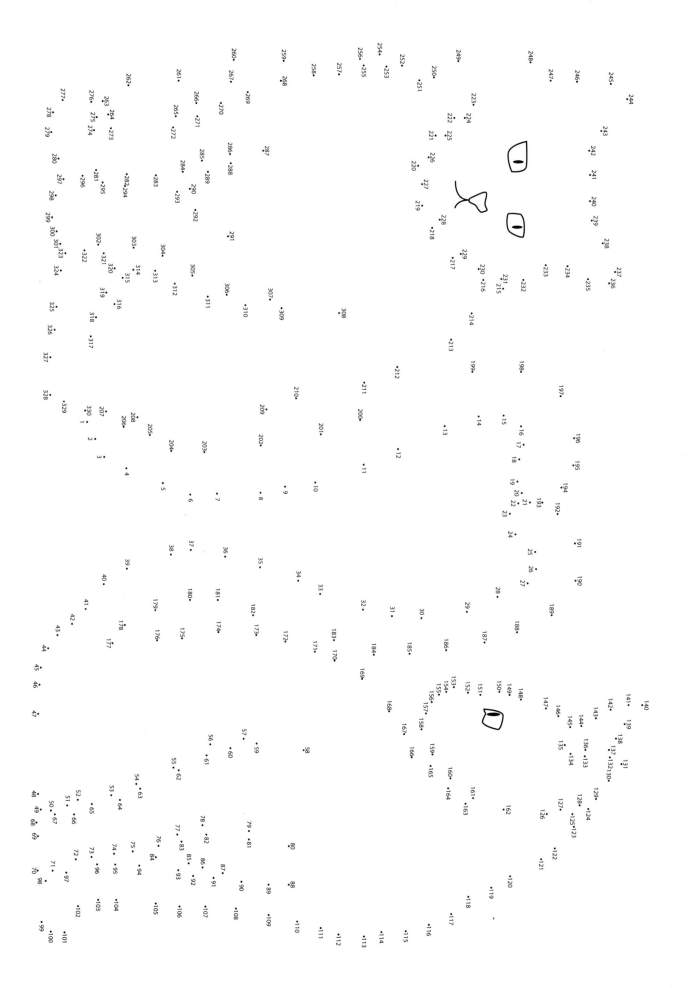

76

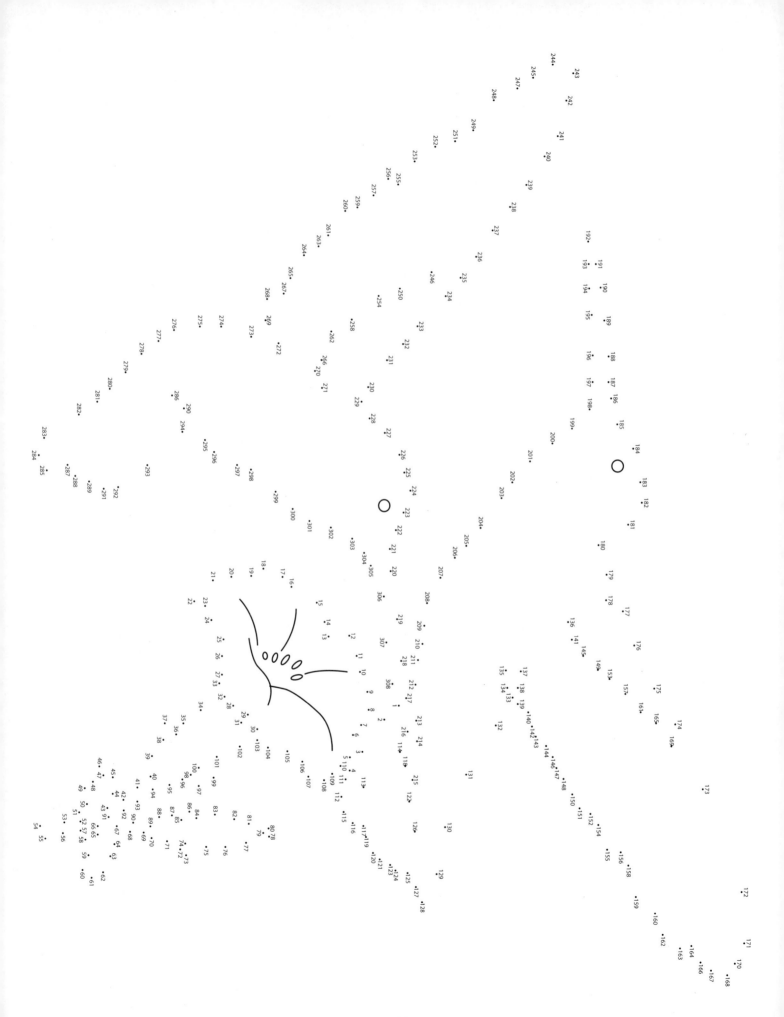

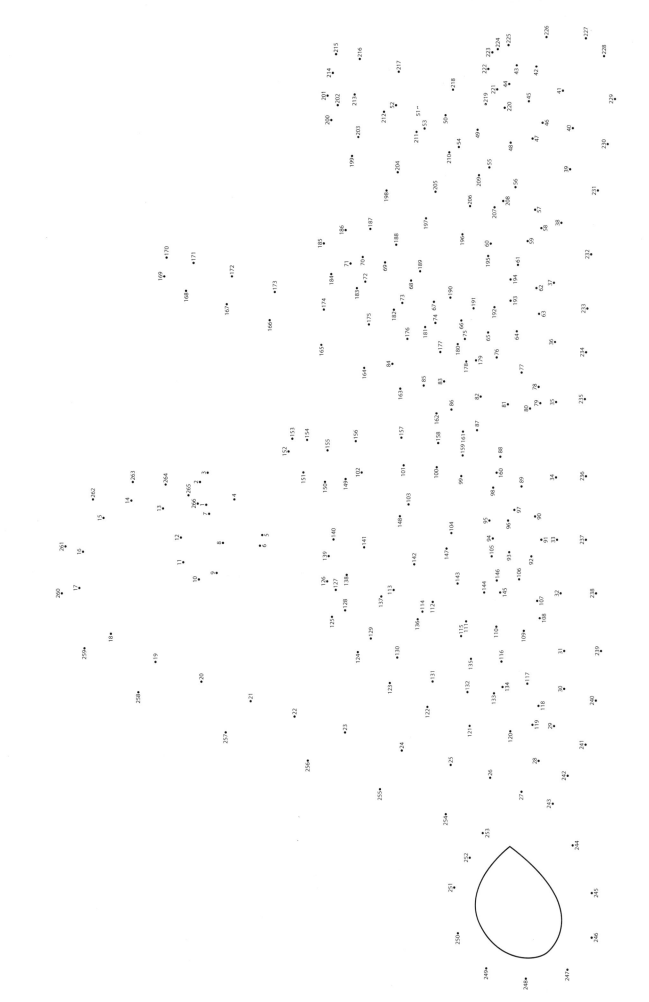

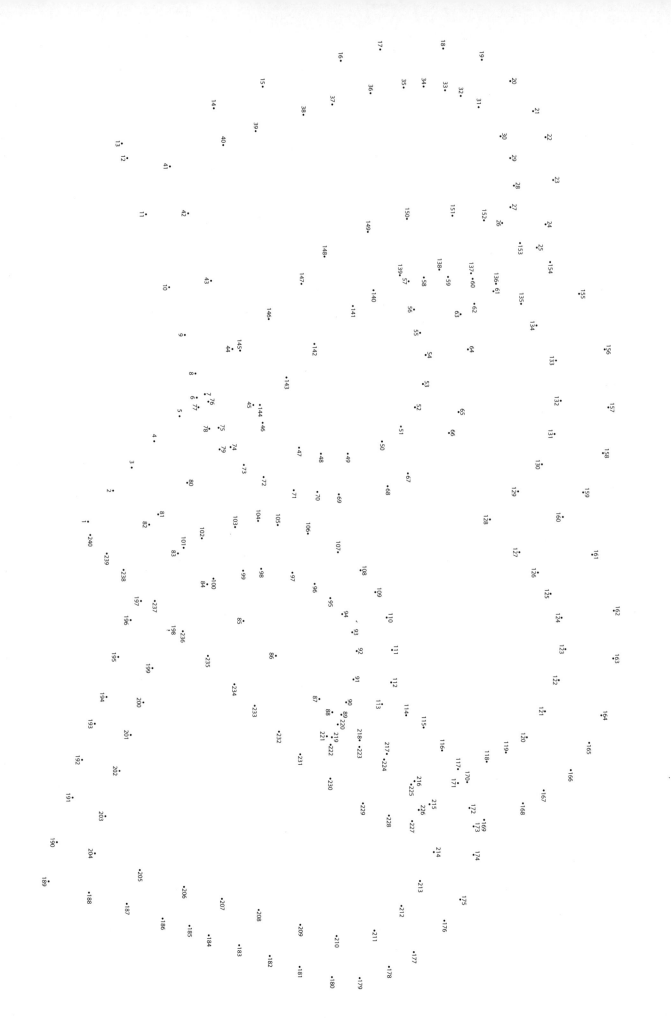

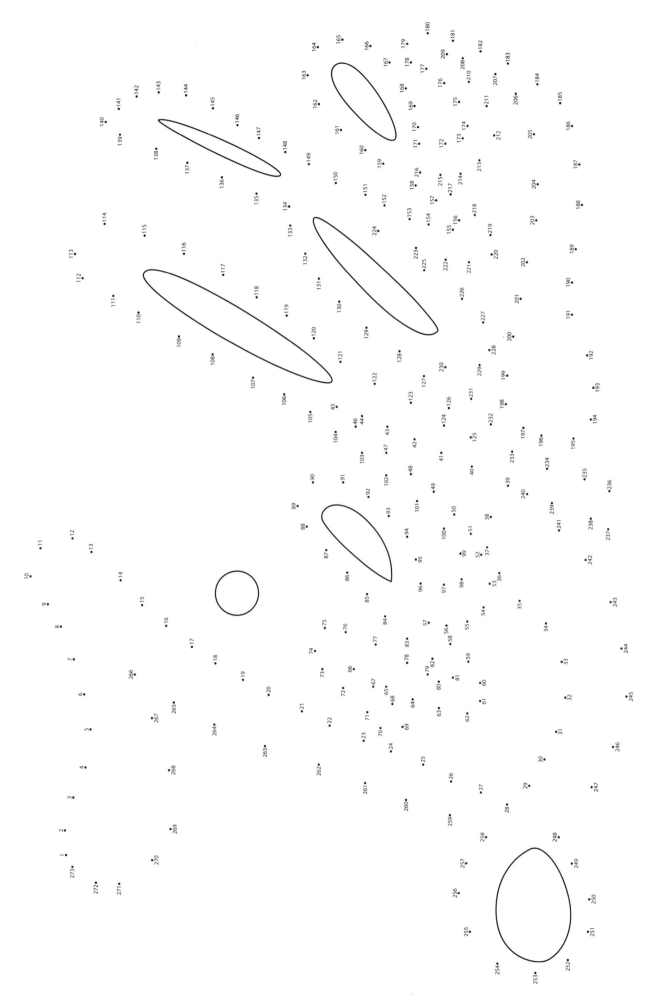

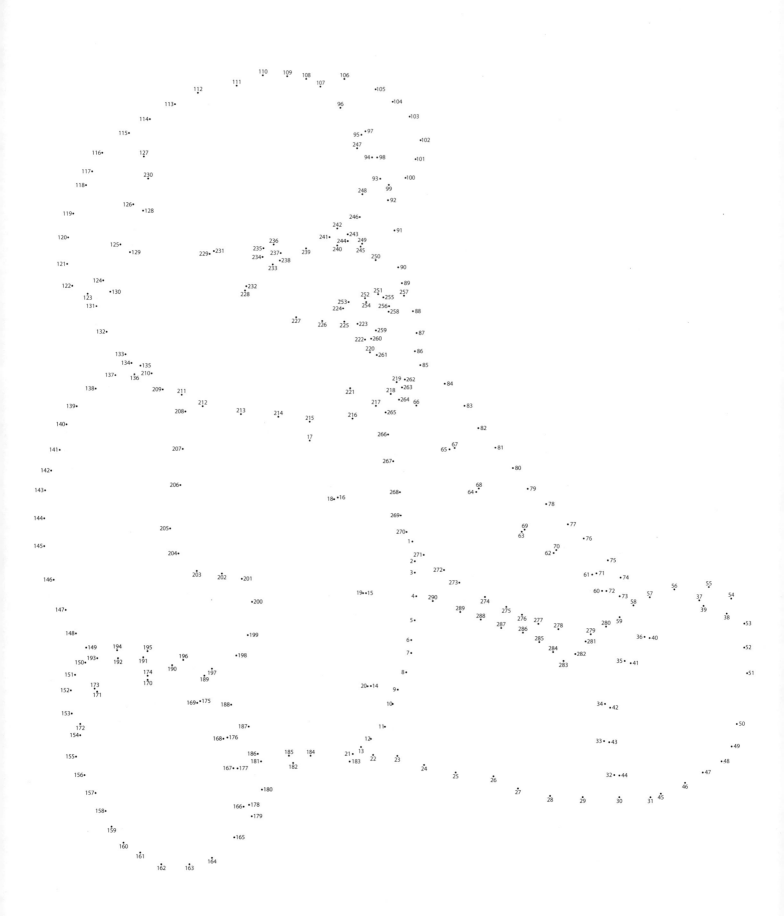

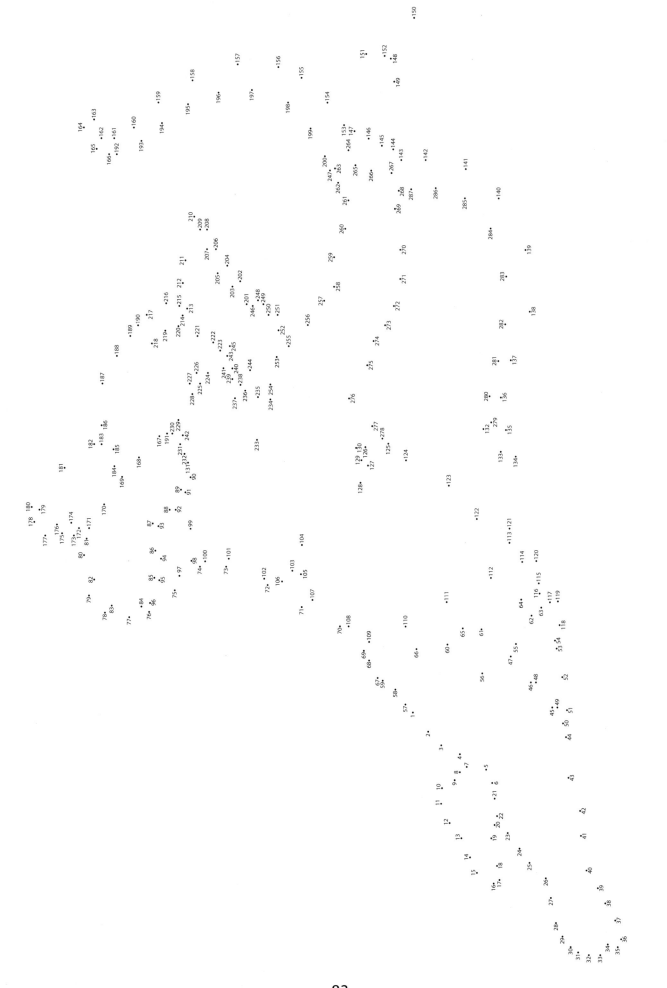

83

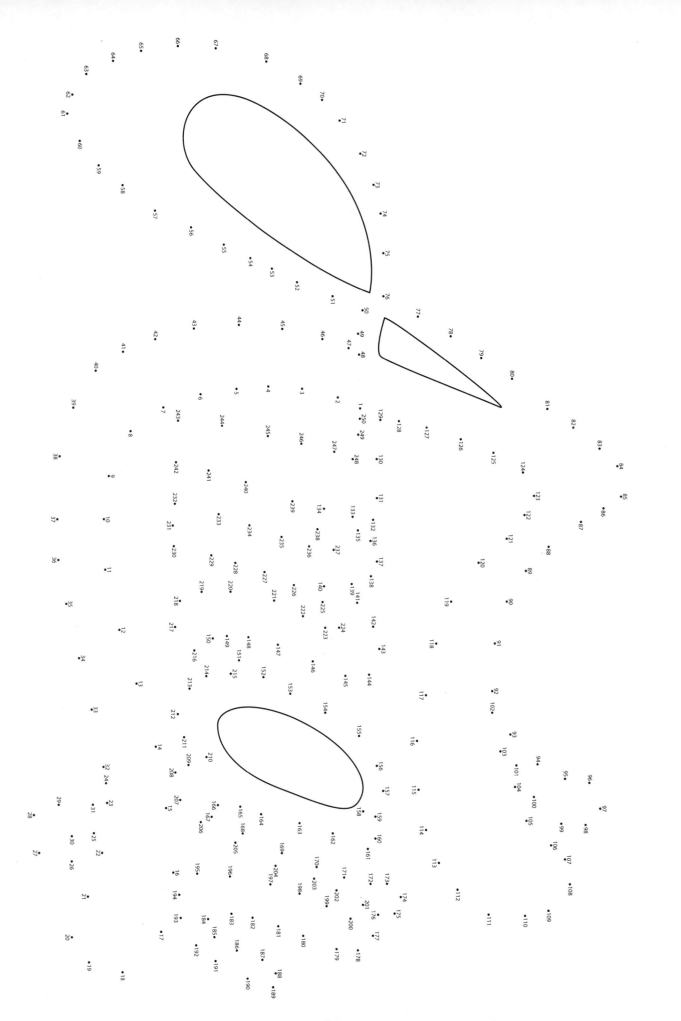

84

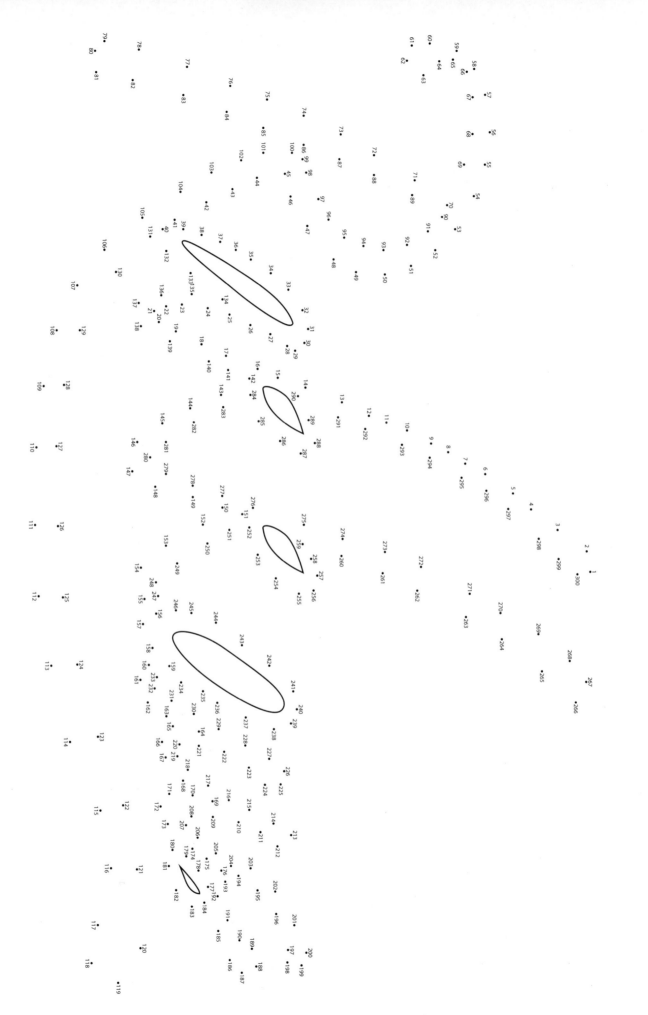

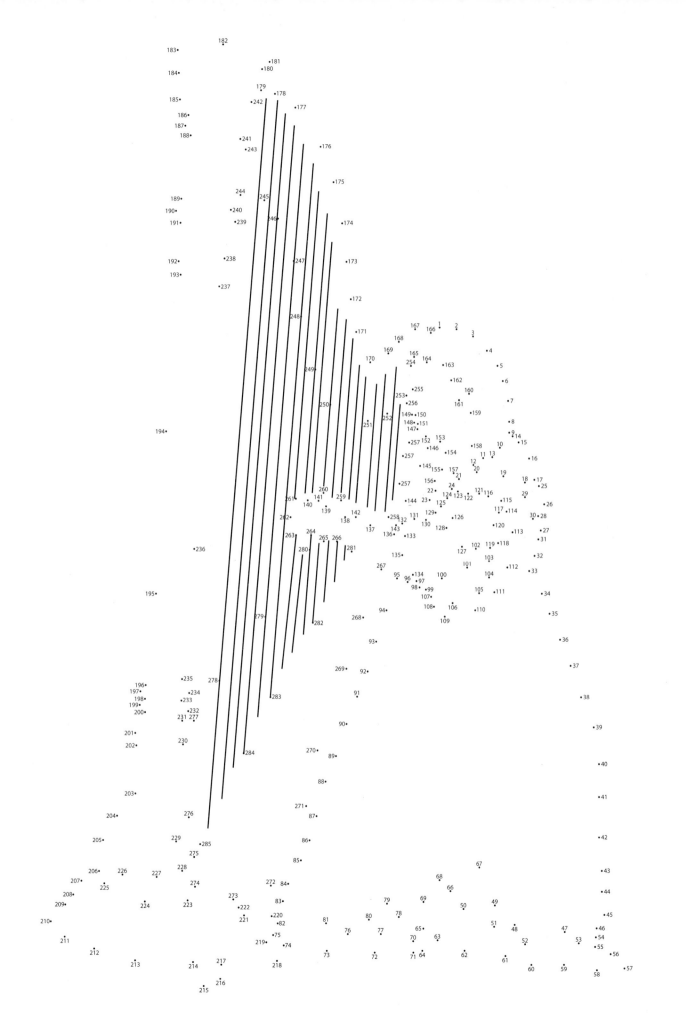

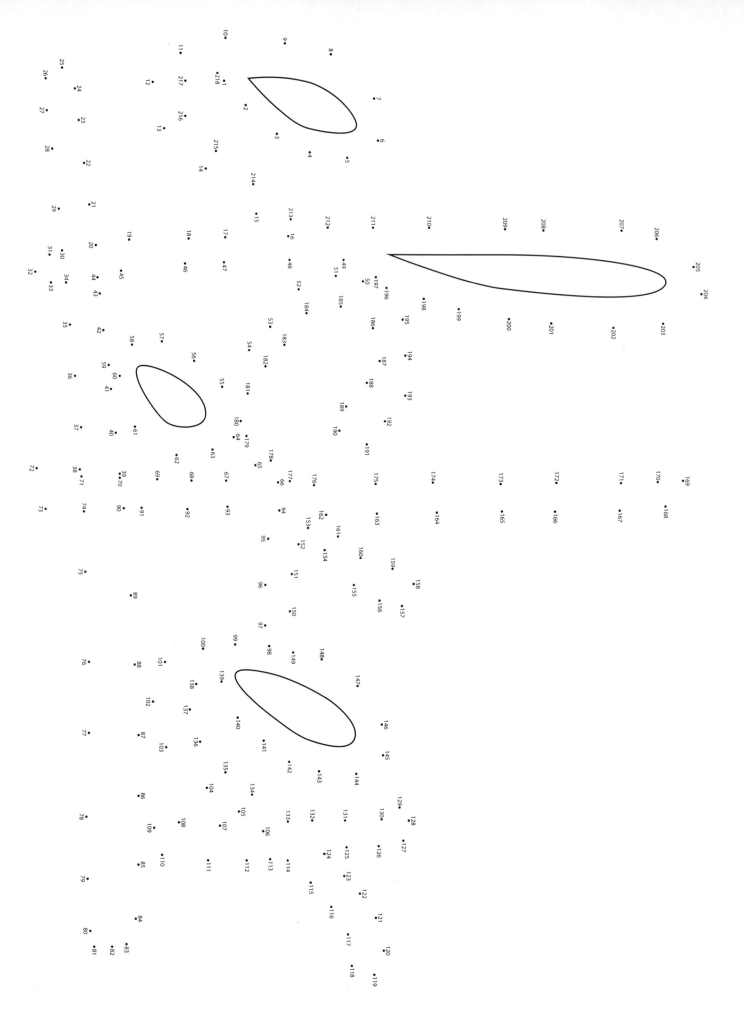

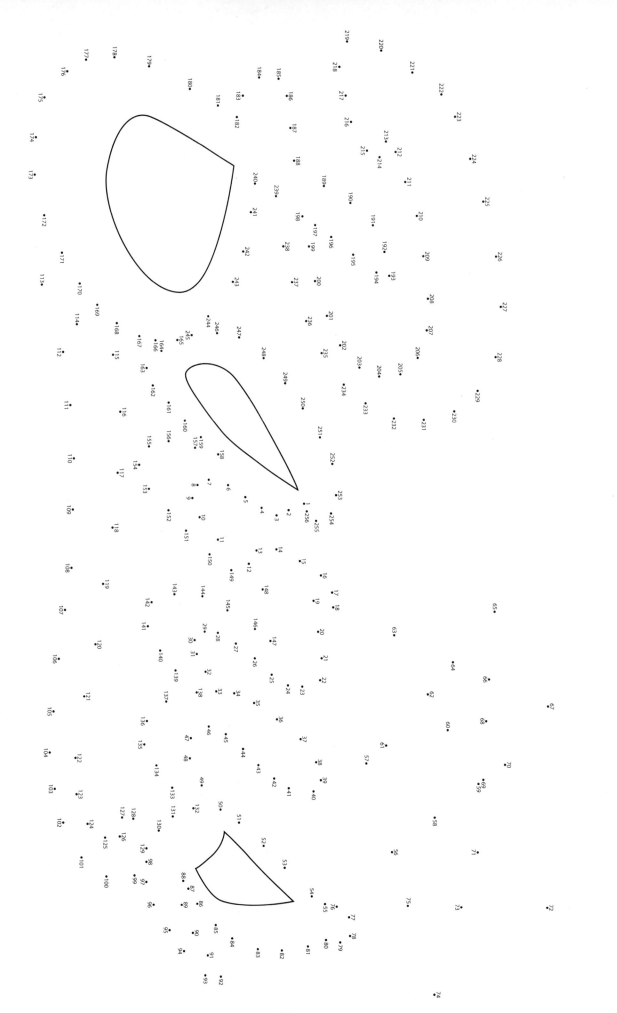

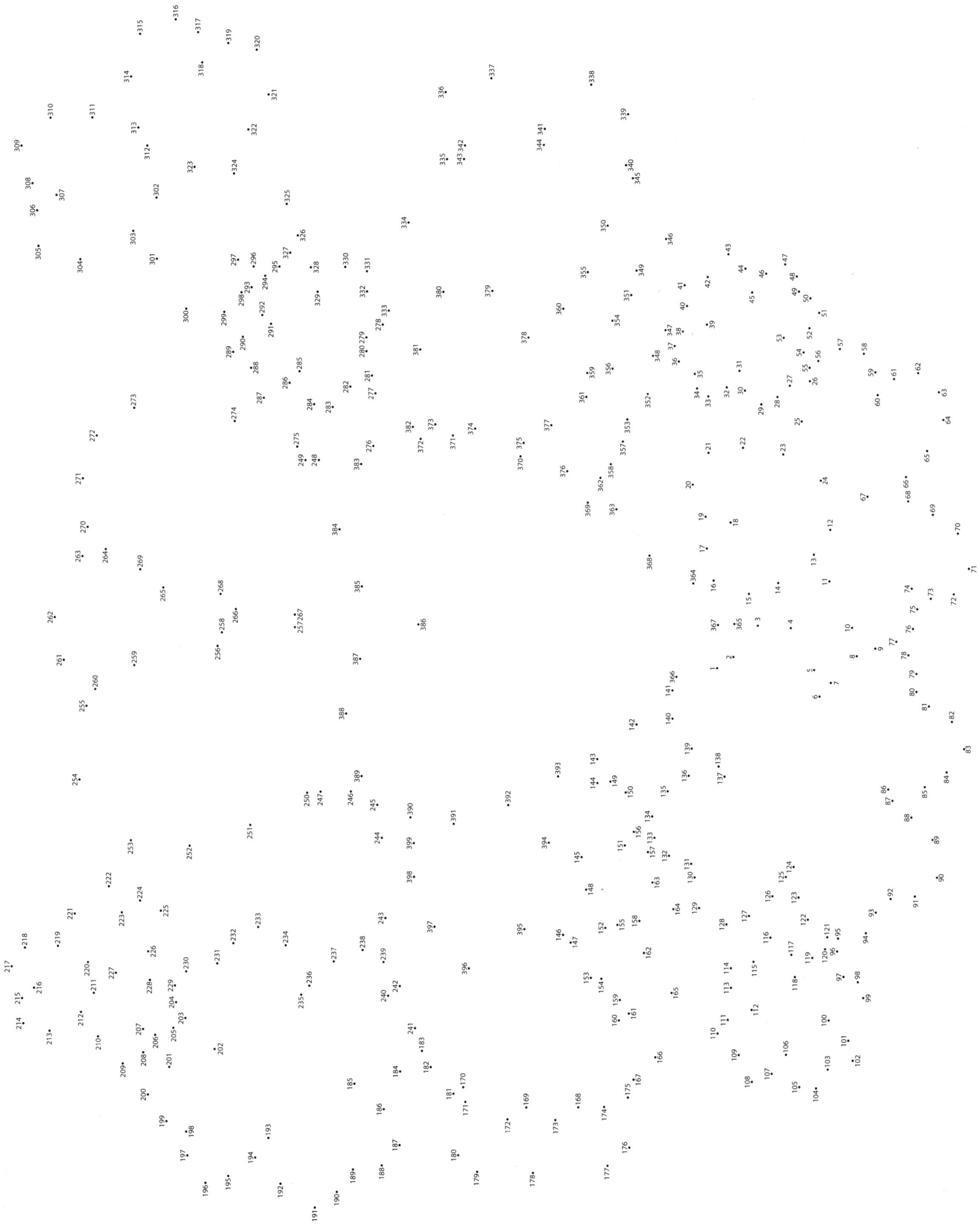

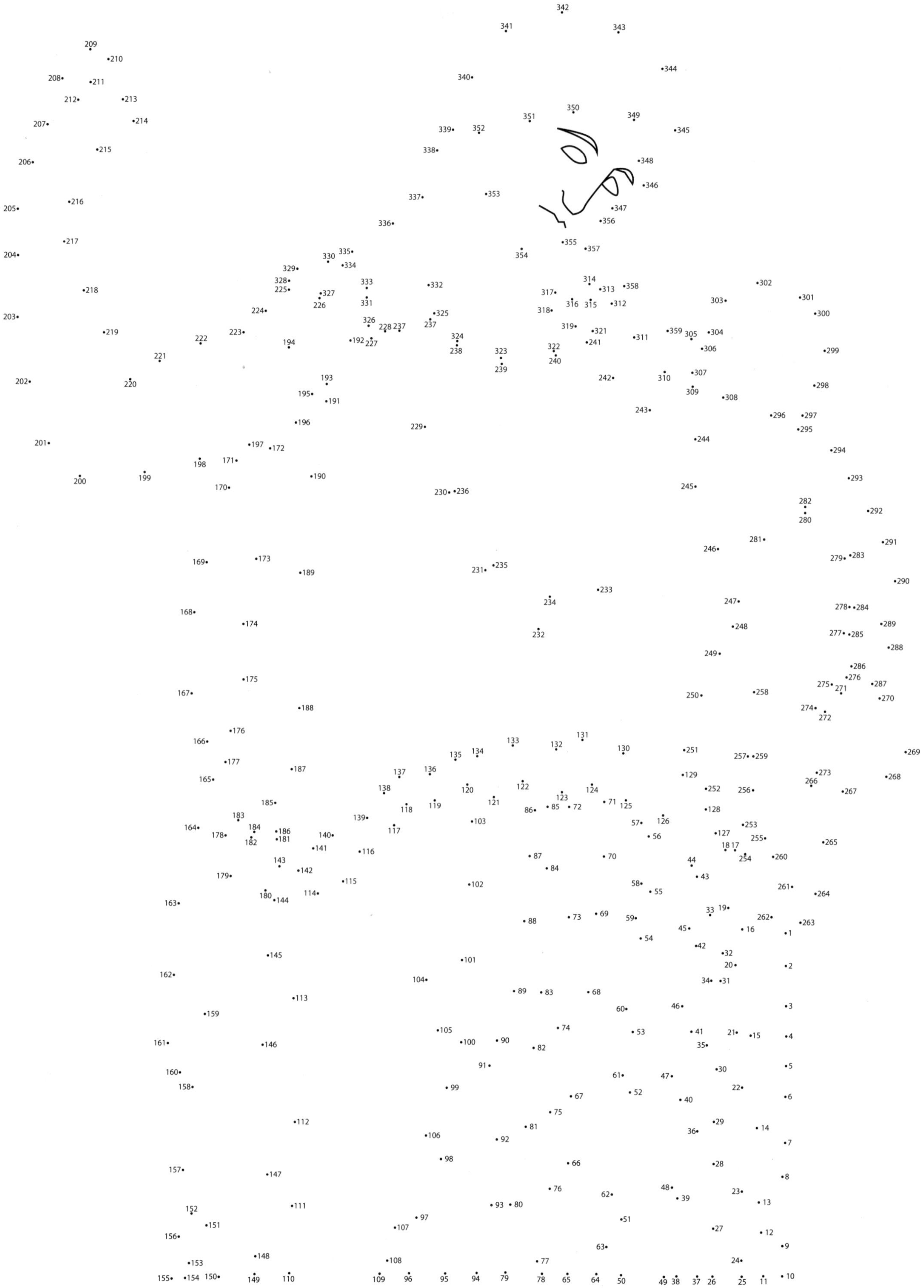

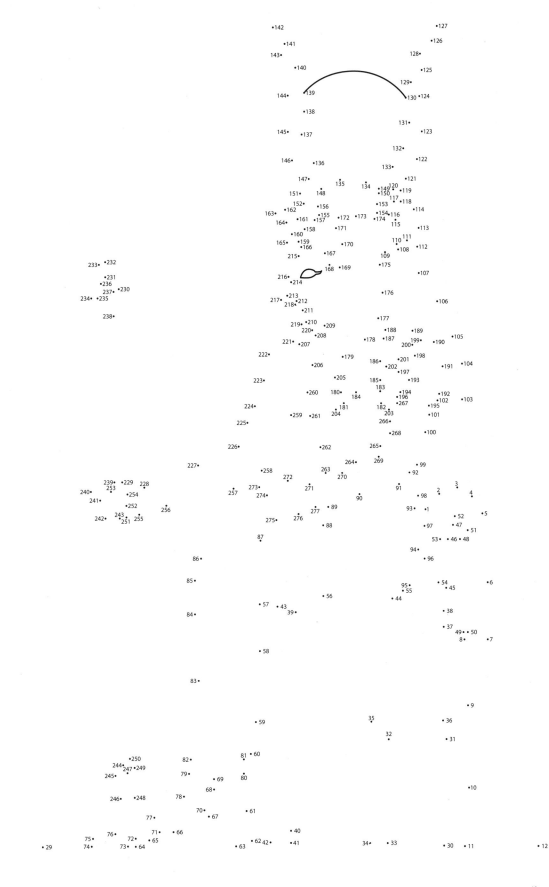

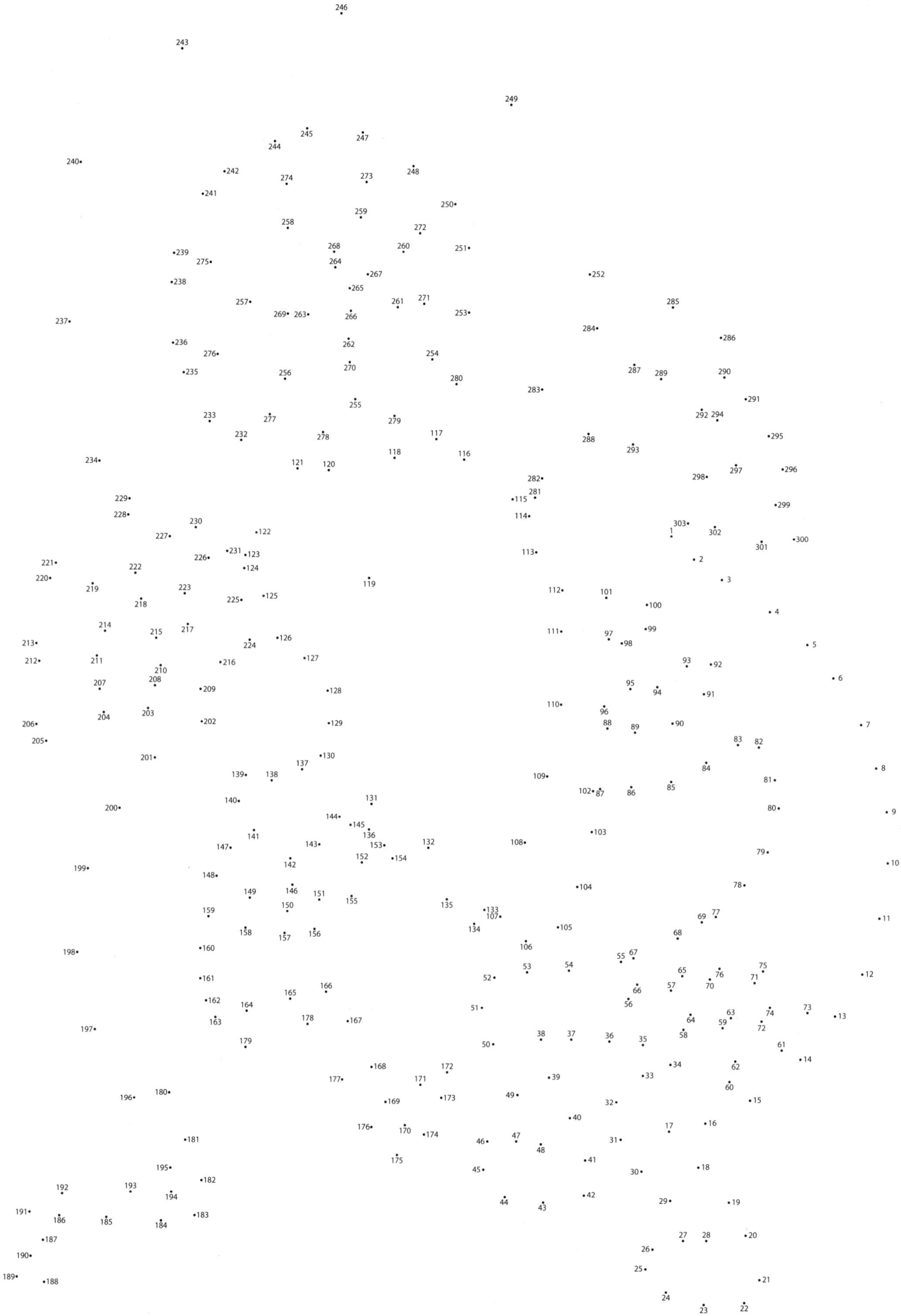

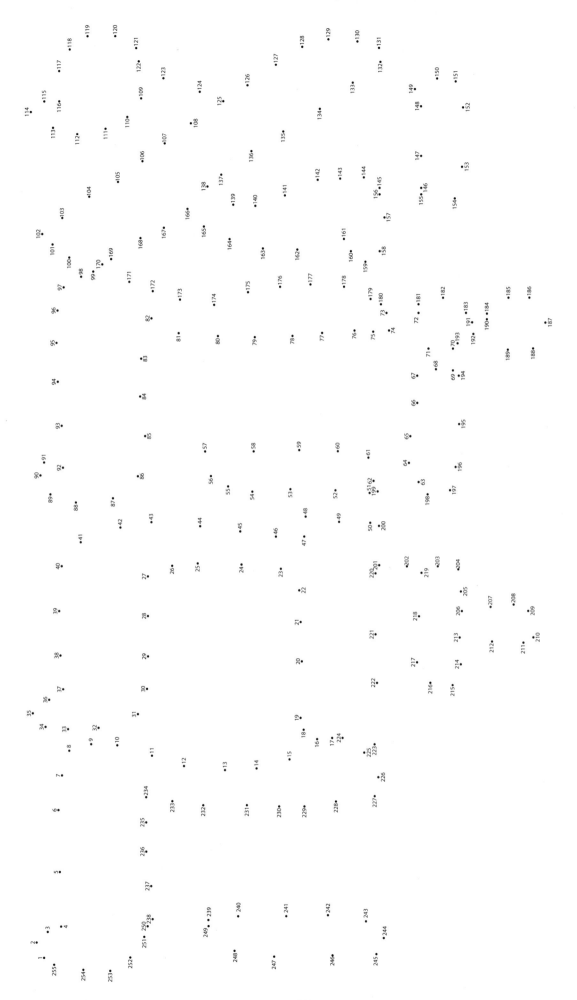

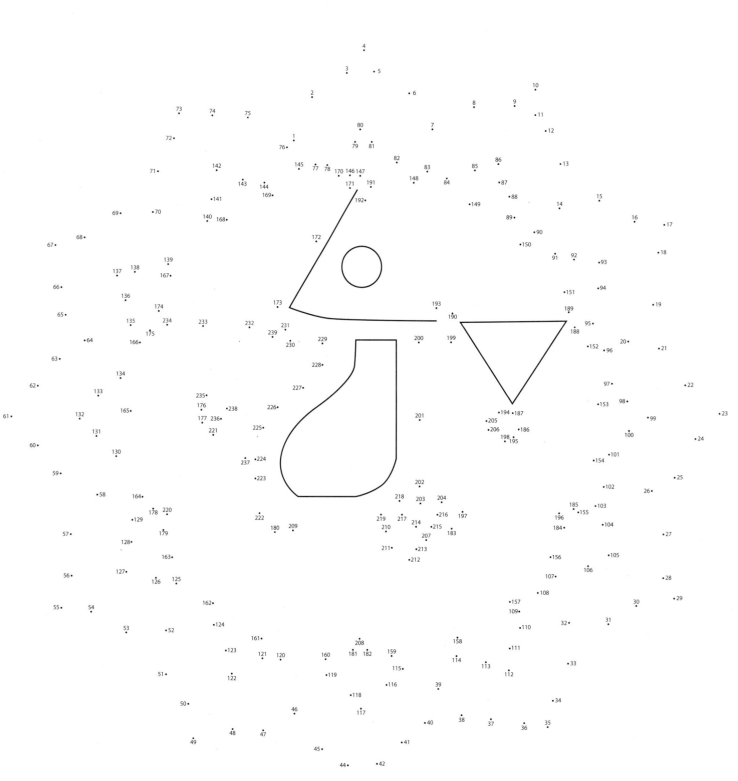

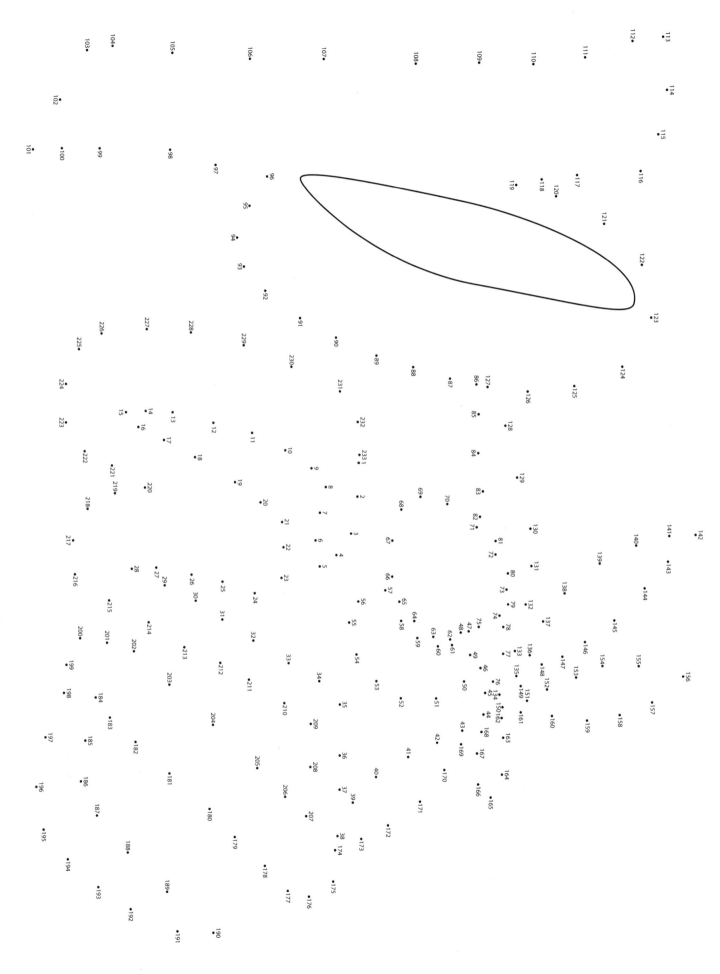

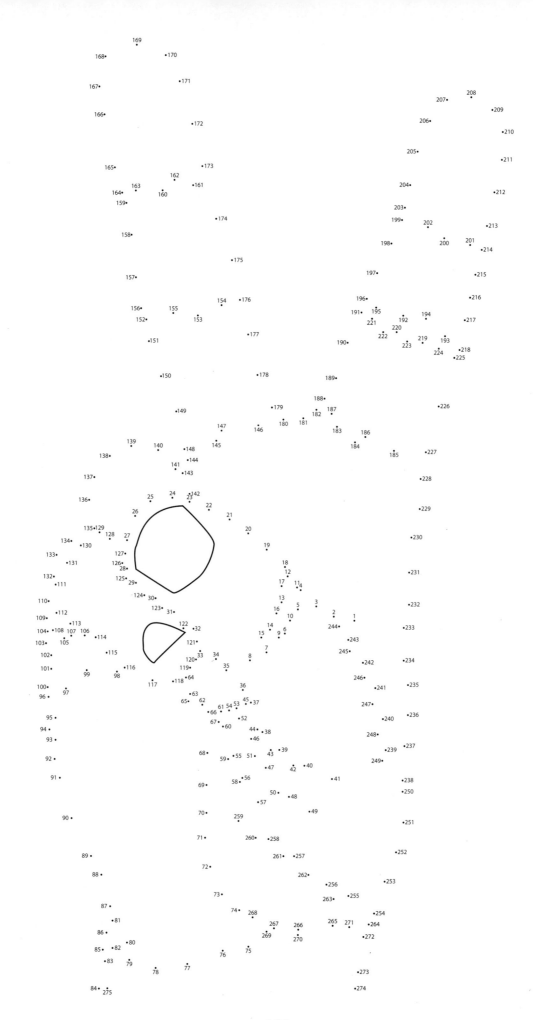

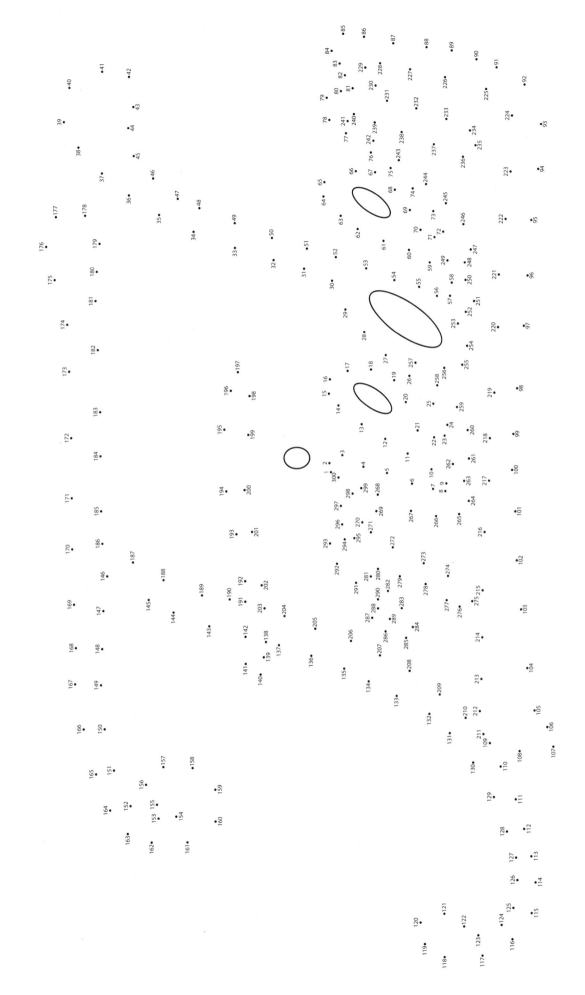

104

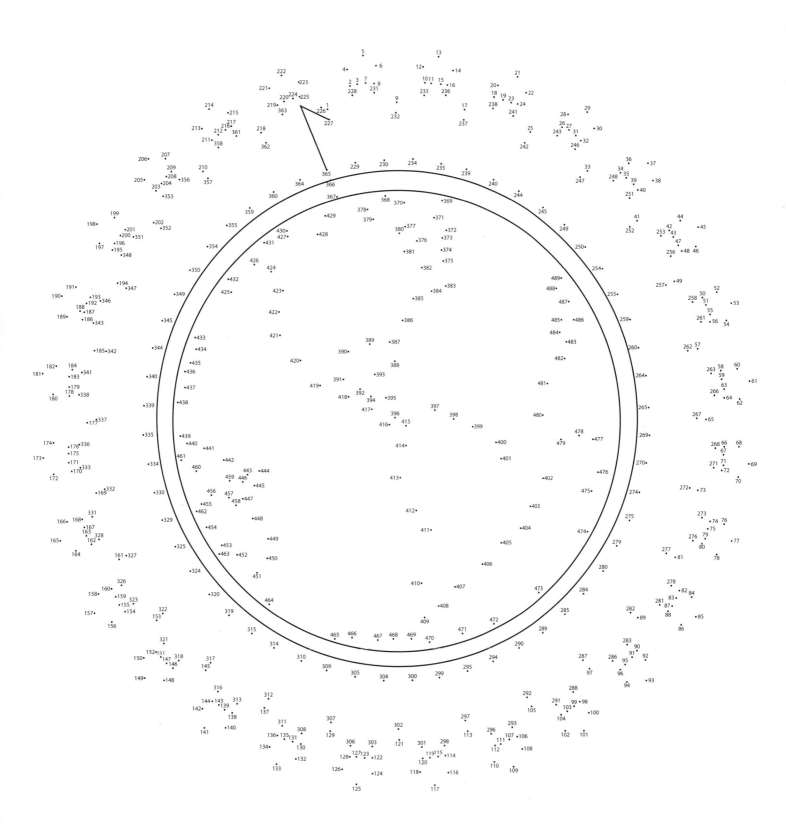

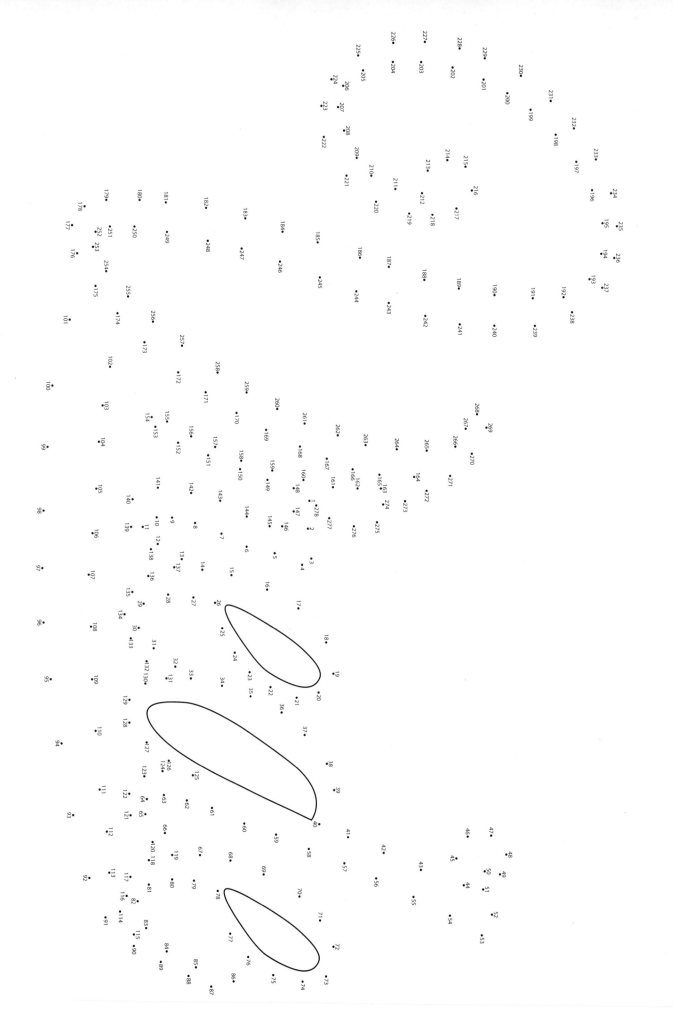

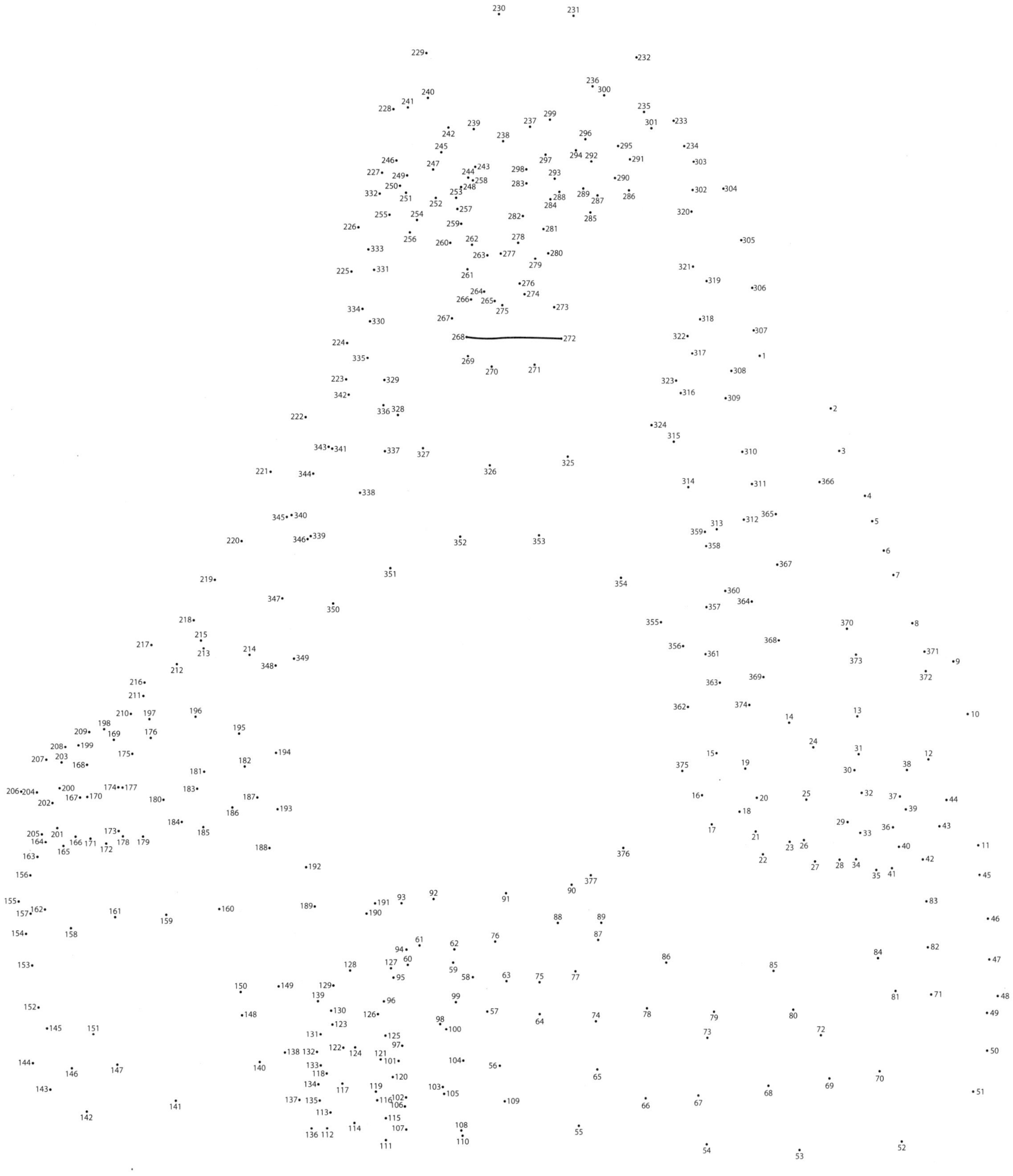

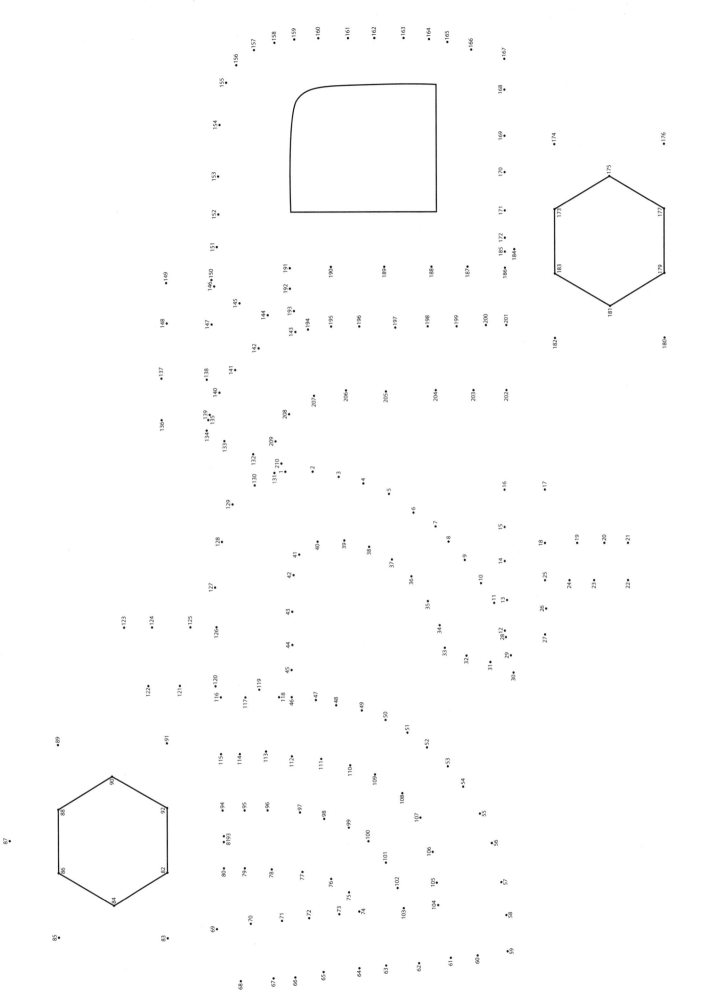

109

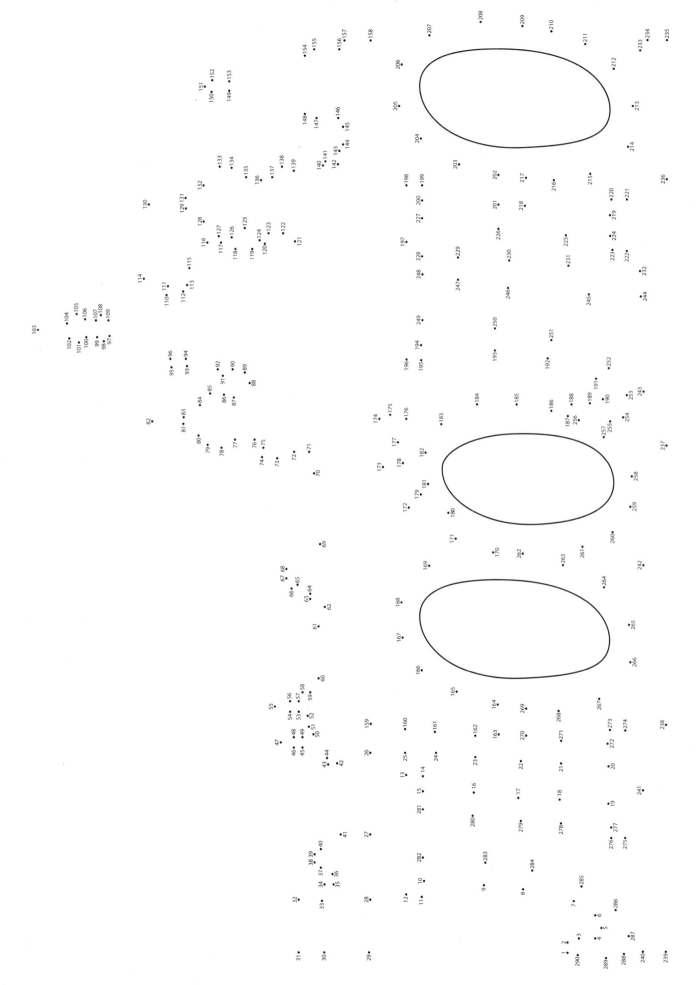

111

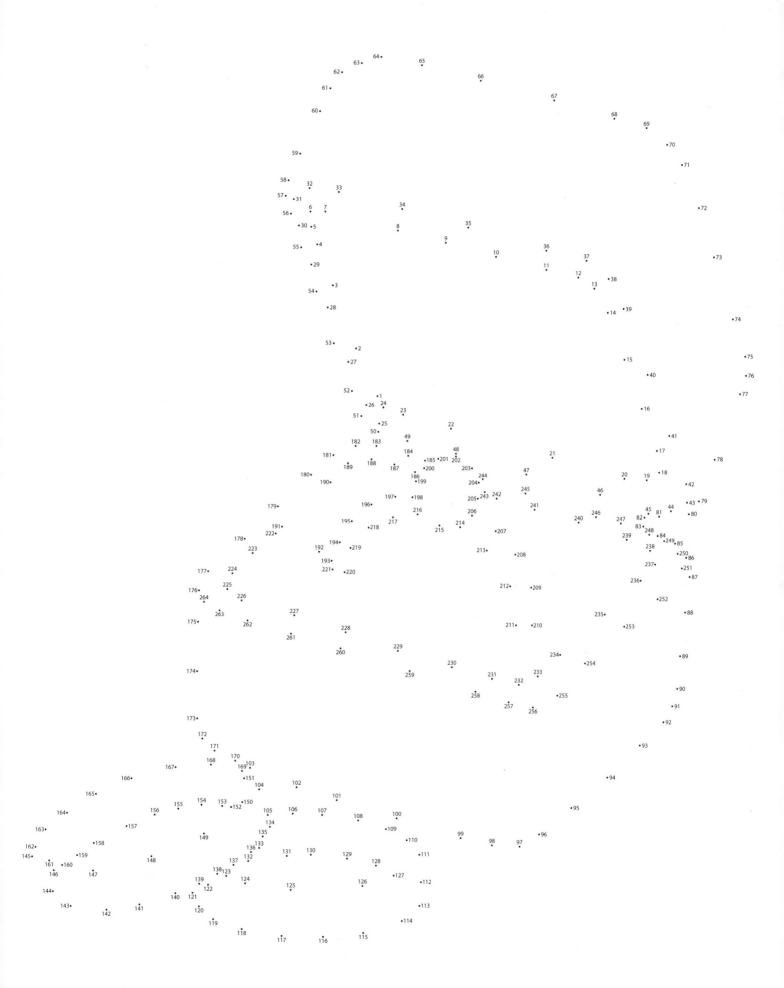

113

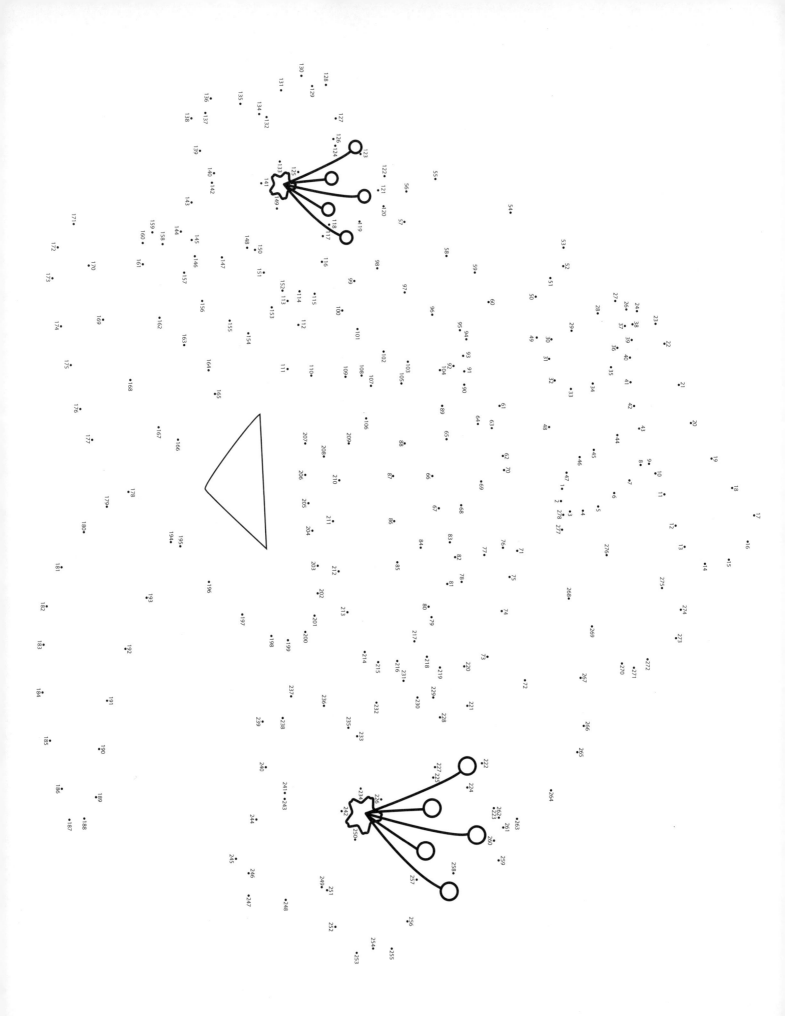

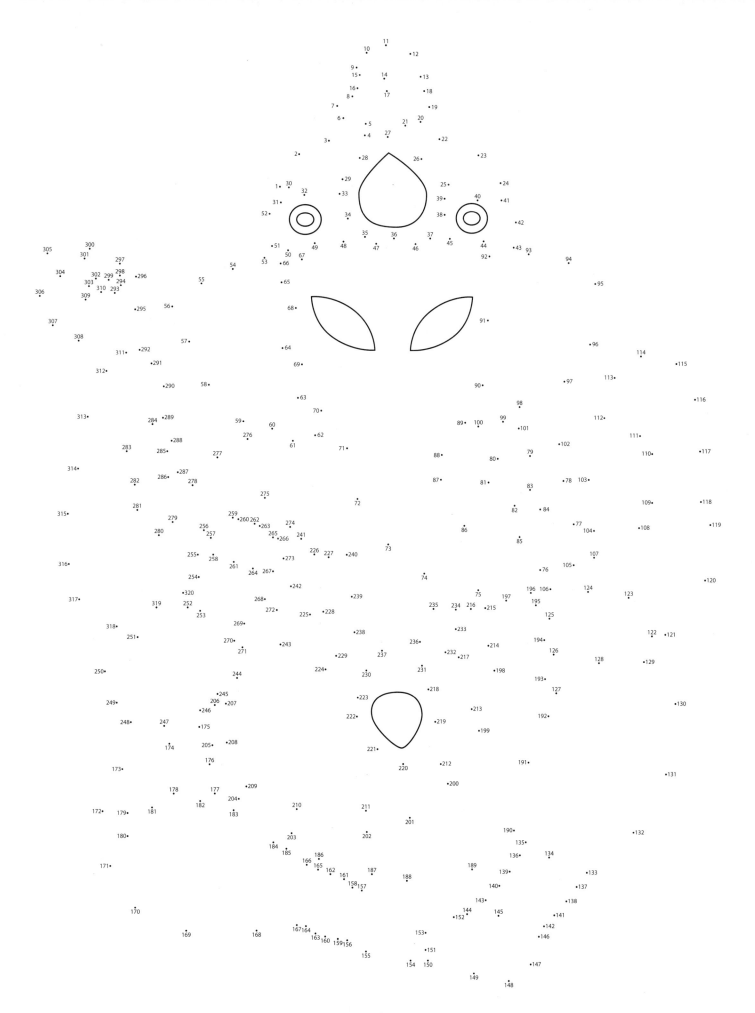

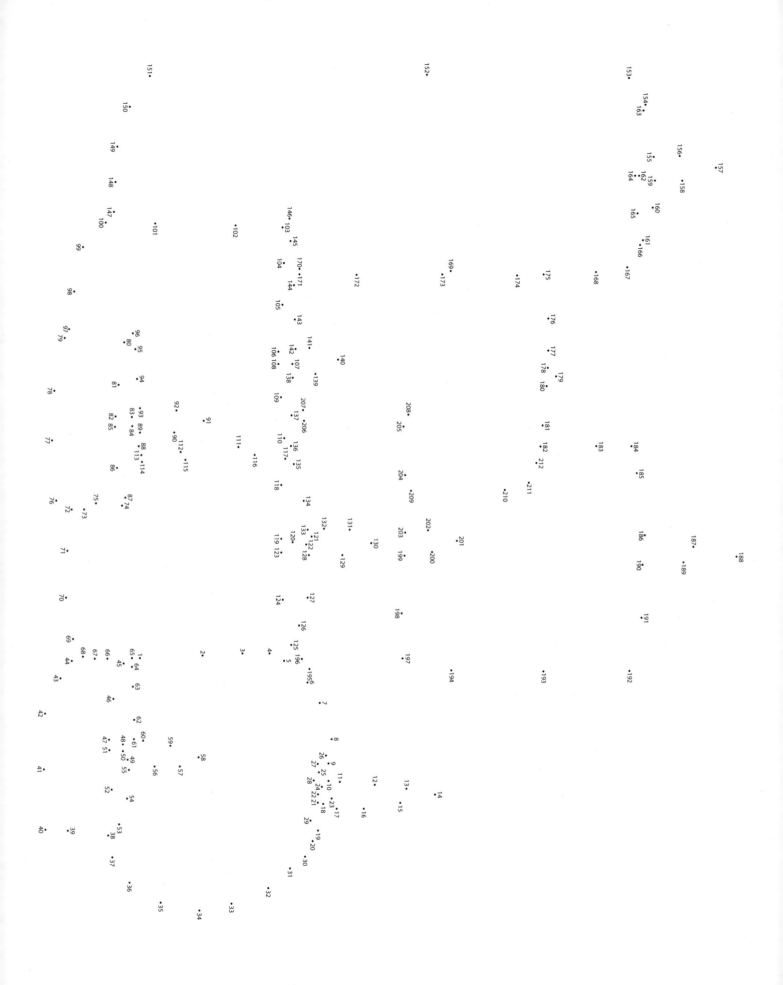

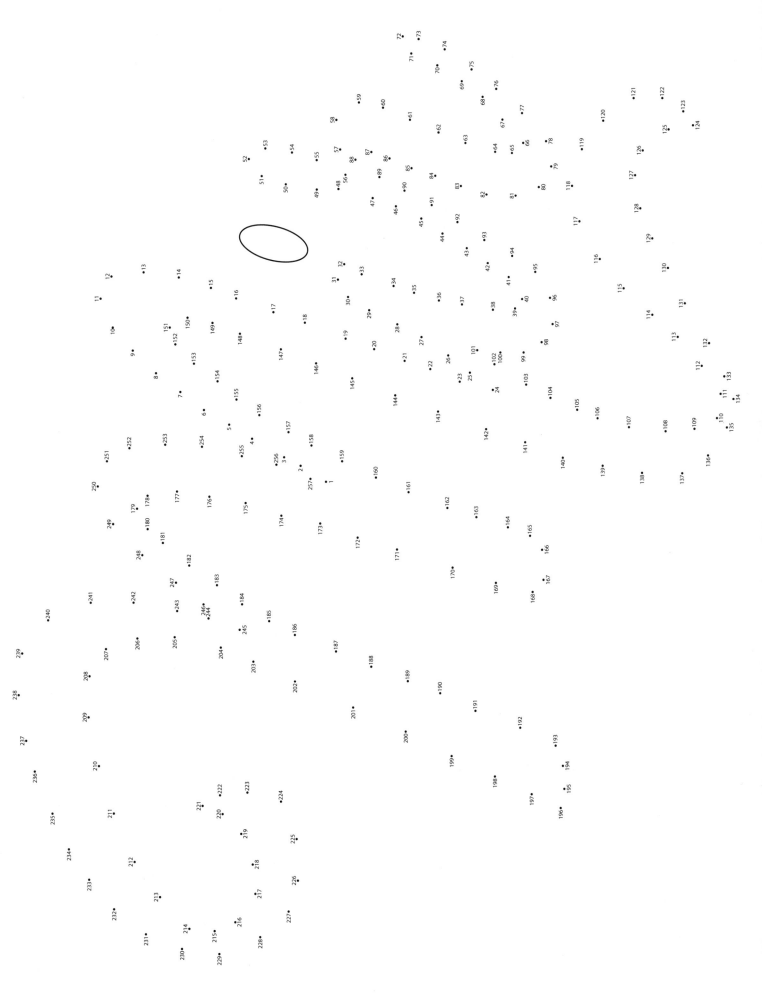

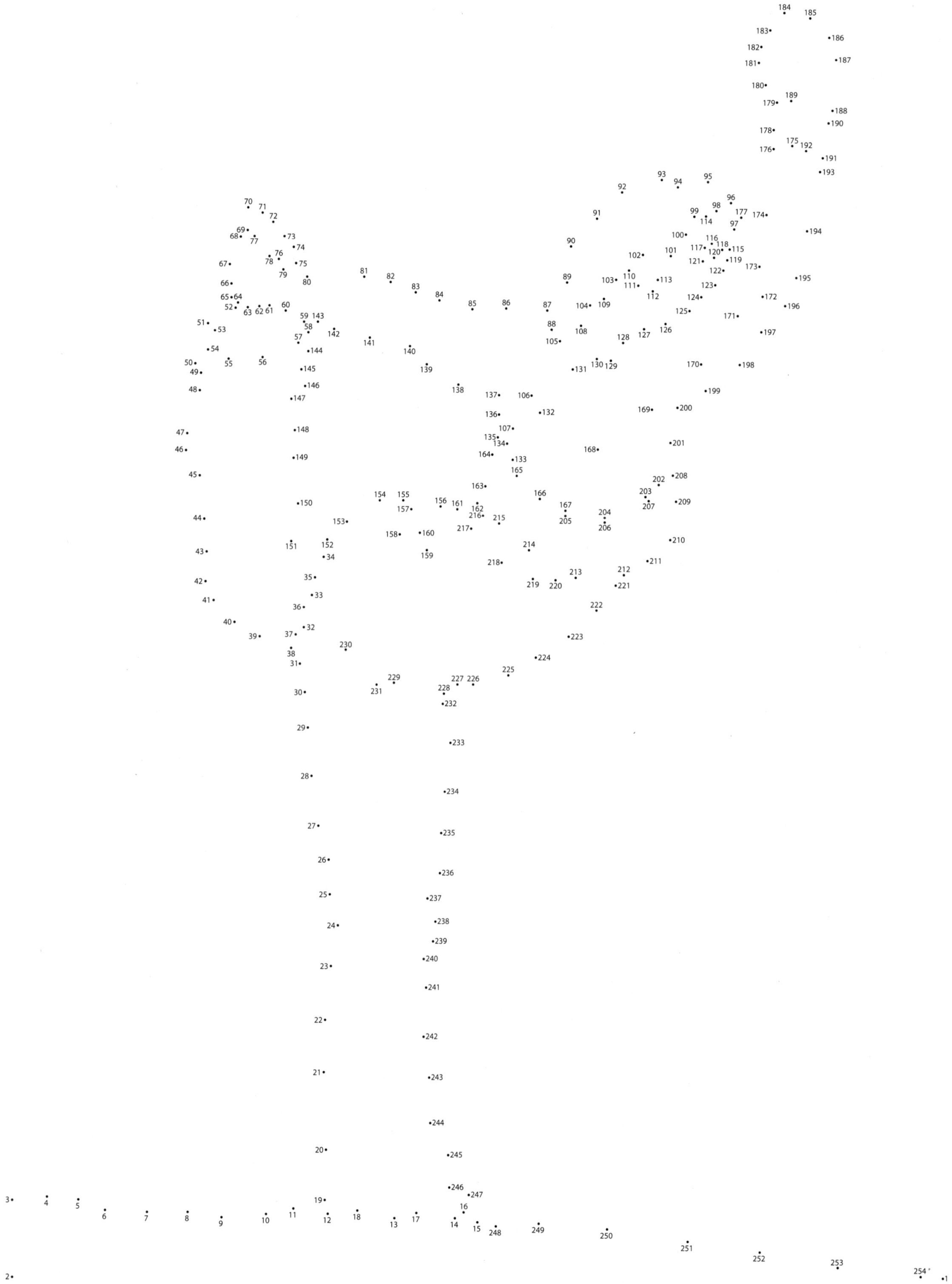

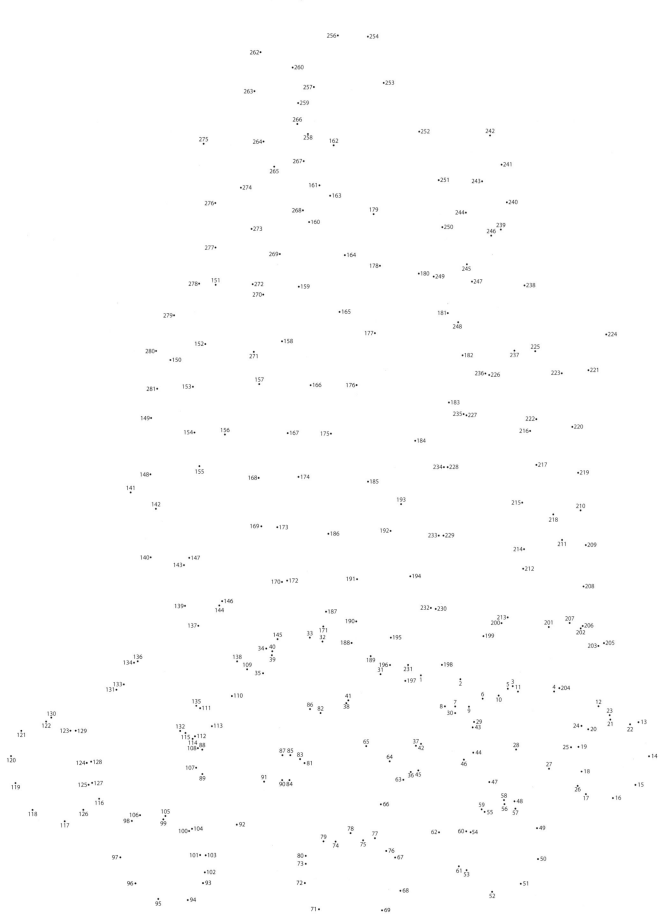

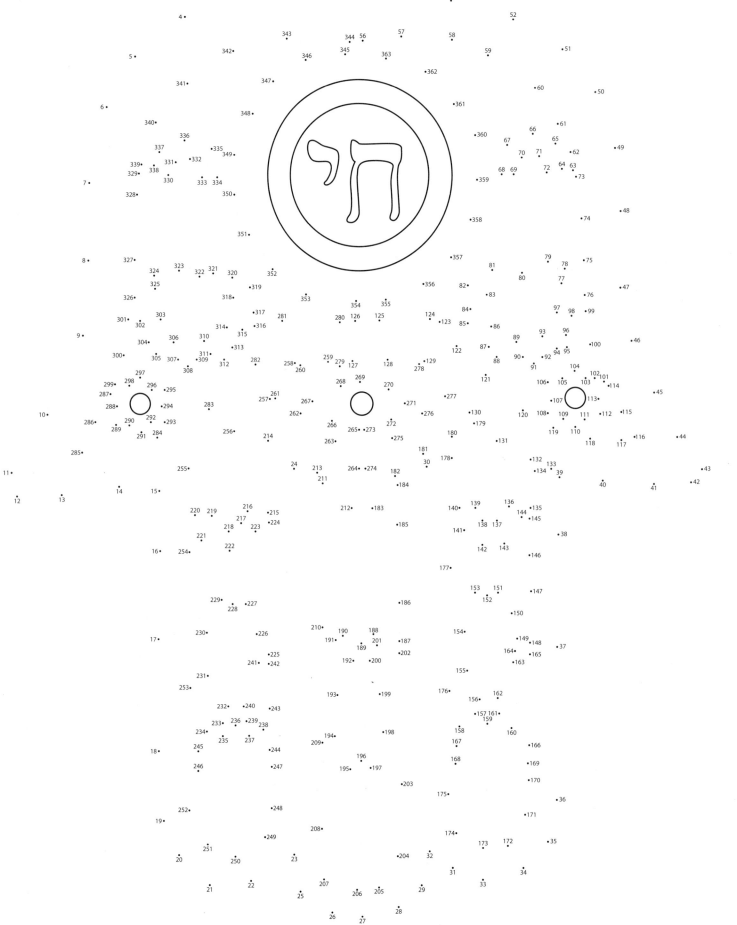

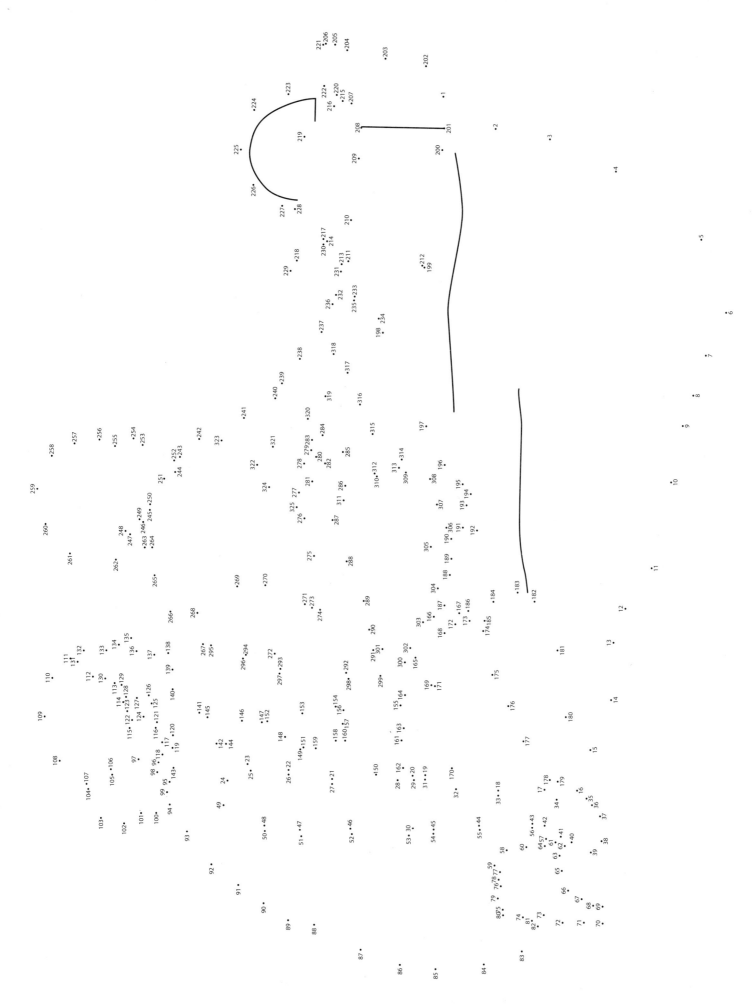

124

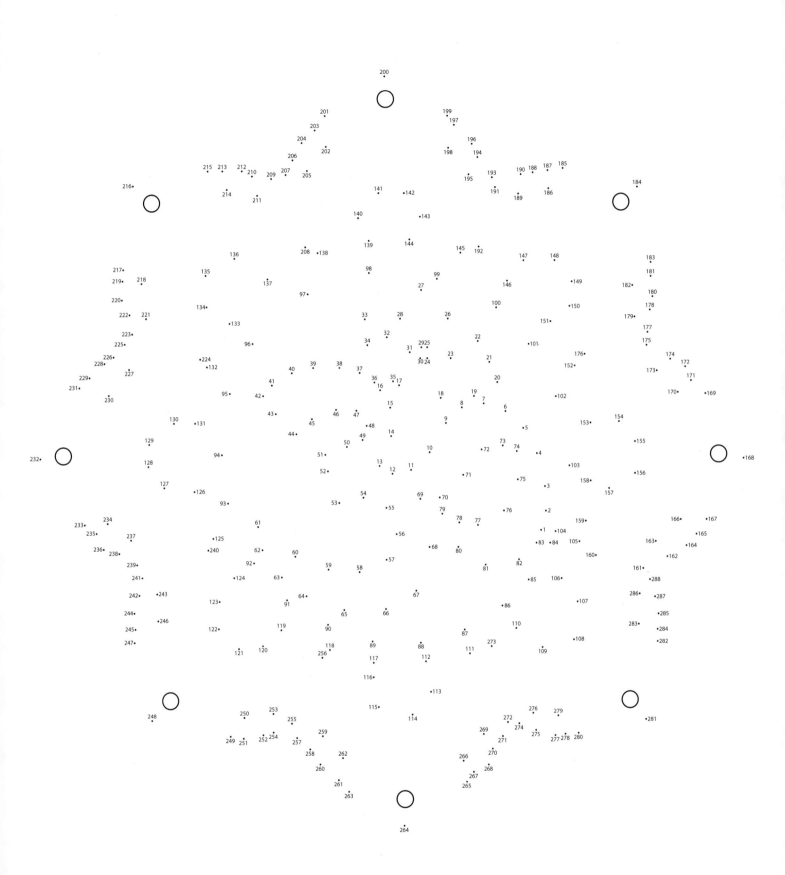

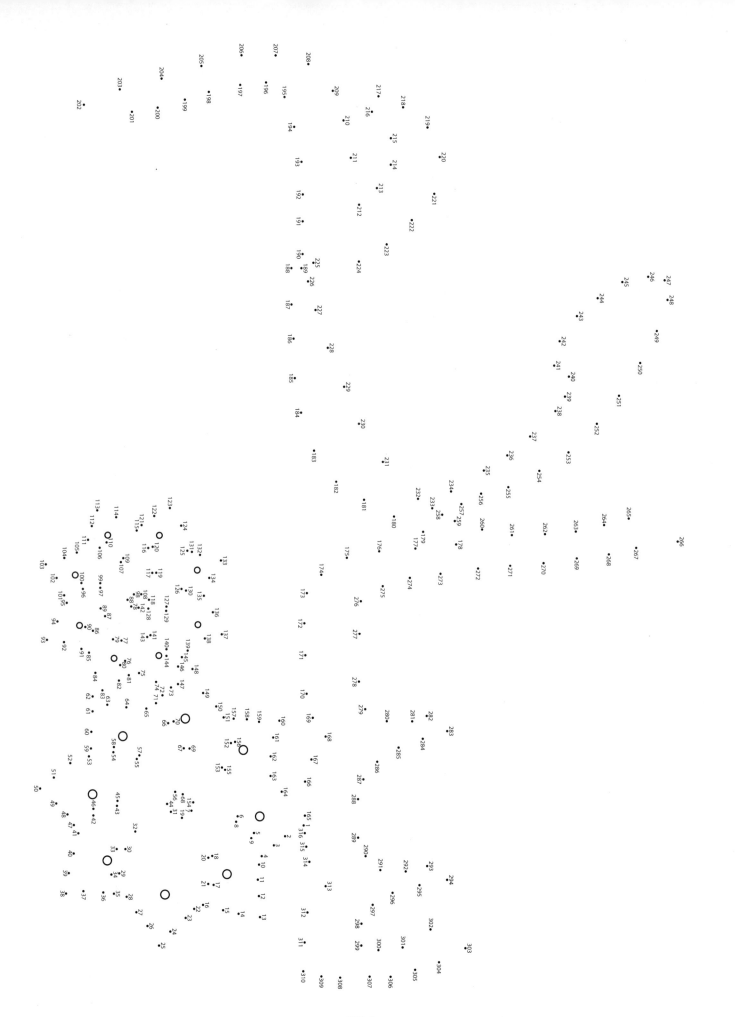

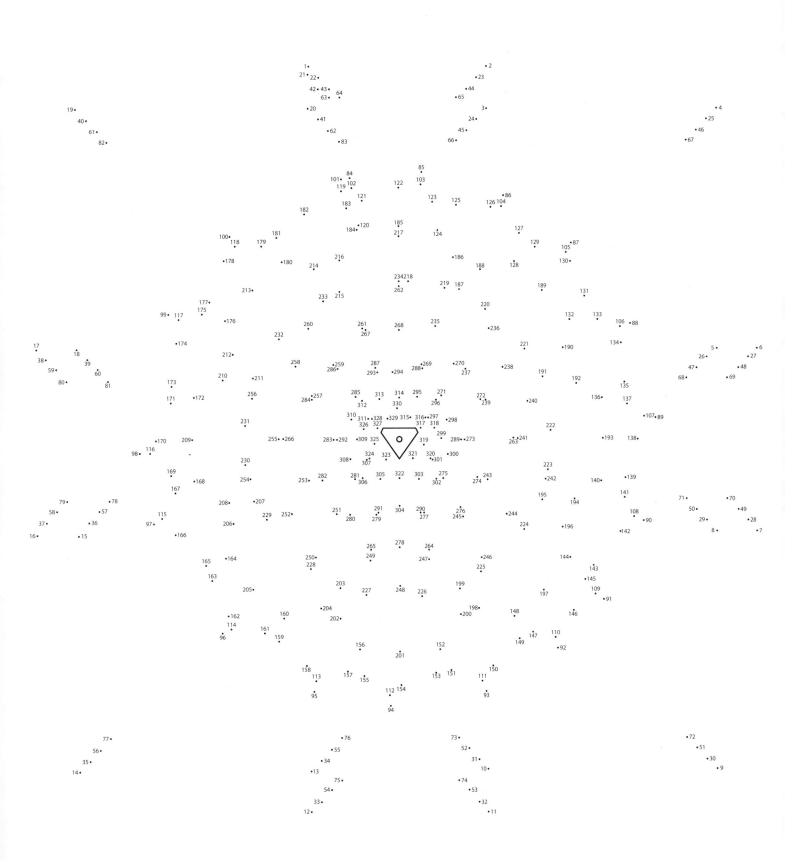

List of Illustrations